Copyright 2020 by Celestina Kent -All rights reserved.

No part of this publication may be reproduced, distributed, or transmitted in any form or by any means, including photocopying, recording, or other electronic or mechanical methods, without the prior written permission of the publisher, except in the case of brief quotations embodied in reviews and certain other non-commercial uses permitted by copyright law.

This Book is provided with the sole purpose of providing relevant information on a specific topic for which every reasonable effort has been made to ensure that it is both accurate and reasonable. Nevertheless, by purchasing this Book you consent to the fact that the author, as well as the publisher, are in no way experts on the topics contained herein, regardless of any claims as such that may be made within. It is recommended that you always consult a professional prior to undertaking any of the advice or techniques discussed within.This is a legally binding declaration that is considered both valid and fair by both the Committee of Publishers Association and the American Bar Association and should be considered as legally binding within the United States.

CONTENTS

Introduction 4
Chapter 1 – Crash Course on Your Air Fryer Toaster Oven 5
Chapter 2 – Breakfast & Brunch 8
    Bacon Ranch Breakfast Bake 8
    Italian Sausage & Egg Taquitos 9
    Strawberry Cheesecake Pastries 10
    Loaded Breakfast Potatoes 11
    Pigs in a Blanket 12
    Apple Fritter Loaf 13
    Enchiladas 4 Breakfast 14
    Cinnamon Streusel Bread 15
    Brioche Breakfast Pudding 16
    Strawberry Basil Muffins 17
Chapter 3 – Fish & Seafood 18
    Salmon Burgers 18
    Air Fried Haddock Filets 19
    Crispy Coated Scallops 20
    Tasty Tuna Loaf 21
    Maryland Crab Cakes 22
    Mediterranean Sole 23
    Coconut Shrimp 24
    Spicy Grilled Halibut 25
    Tropical Shrimp Skewers 26
    Seafood Mac n Cheese 27
Chapter 4 – Beef, Lamb & Pork 28
    Pork Wellington 28
    Garlic Infused Roast Beef 29
    Stuffed Pork Loin 30
    Beef Chimichangas 31
    Chinese BBQ Pork 32
    Tender Baby Back Ribs 33
    Crispy Lamb Chops 34
    Garlic Butter Pork Chops 35
    Honey BBQ Lamb Chops 36
    Country Fried Steak 37
    Pork Schnitzel 38
    Stuffed Bell Peppers 39
    Mixed Meat Balls 40
    Dijon Roasted Lamb Chops 41
    Spiced Pork Roast 42
Chapter 5- Poultry 43
    Buffalo Chicken Tenders 43
    Turkey Turnovers 44
    Chicken Parm 45

Teriyaki Duck Legs ... 46
Turkey Burgers ... 47
Spicy Chicken Nuggets ... 48
Turkey Meatloaf ... 49
Lacquered Duck Breasts ... 50
Copycat Chicken Sandwich ... 51
Mini Pot Pies ... 52
Popcorn Turkey ... 53
Italian Chicken Casserole ... 54
Roast Duck ... 55
Sweet & Spicy Chicken ... 56
Guacamole Stuffed Chicken ... 57

Chapter 6 – Vegetarian & Vegan ... 58
Crispy Potato Lentil Nuggets ... 58
Portobello Steaks ... 59
Vegan Meatloaf ... 60
Teriyaki Tofu ... 61
Butter Burgers ... 62
Spaghetti Squash Lasagna ... 63
Green Chili Taquitos ... 64
Chickpea Fritters ... 65
Roasted Fall Veggies ... 66
Asian Tofu "Meatballs" ... 67

Chapter 7 - Desserts ... 68
Cinnamon Cheesecake Bars ... 68
Strawberry Cobbler ... 69
Banana Brownies ... 70
Caramel Apple Cake ... 71
Rocky Road Squares ... 72
Cappuccino Blondies ... 73
Mini Pecan Pies ... 74
Churros with Chocolate Dipping Sauce ... 75
Simple Cinnamon Rolls ... 76
Crispy Coated Peaches ... 77

Chapter 8 – Snacks & Appetizers ... 78
Beef Enchilada Dip ... 78
Cheesy Stuffed Sliders ... 79
Philly Egg Rolls ... 80
Mozzarella Cheese Sticks ... 81
Buffalo Quesadillas ... 82
Crispy Sausage Bites ... 83
Puffed Asparagus Spears ... 84
Wonton Poppers ... 85
Party Pull Apart ... 86
Easy Cheesy Stuffed Mushrooms ... 87

Introduction

I love trying and collecting kitchen gadgets almost as much as I love cooking. Lately, I have been seeing commercials for this new Cuisinart Air Fryer Toaster Oven and I thought, "Oh, that looks like fun" So, of course, I bought one! I couldn't wait to get it home to see what I could cook and bake in it.

Once I started using it, I couldn't stop. This compact oven does everything my old one did, but it uses less electricity and offers more options on how to cook your food. Like most Americans, I am a big fan of fried foods. However, I am not a fan of all those greasy calories. The fact that this oven has a built-in air fryer was a big selling point indeed.

I started with some of the recipes that came with the oven, but I quickly got bored with those. While they are good recipes, I consider myself a bit more of a gourmet in the kitchen. So, I got busy adapting some of my fancier and fun dishes to work with this new-fangled cooker. And I got to thinking, if I want a bigger variety of recipes then other folks would too. That is where this cookbook comes in.

I decided to put together a cookbook that anyone can use, even beginners. You will notice that all the recipes I included have easy-to-follow instructions. Like many people, I try to watch what I eat and I don't like to work with a lot of processed foods. All of these recipes use common, easy to find ingredients without a lot of additives or preservatives.

In keeping with the latest health trends and diets, the recipes also include complete nutrition information. Unlike many recipes, you will see the information listed includes potassium and phosphorus, which most cooks don't list. While these recipes do use real, whole foods, they have not been created for folks on a diet.

This cookbook is for people who want to create tasty dishes without spending all day in the kitchen. Most of the recipes can be prepared in 15 minutes or less. And most of them can be on the table in under an hour. With today's busy lifestyles, I know this is important to most of you.

I have broken down the chapters by categories of meals. For example, breakfast and brunch, desserts, and snacks and appetizers. I have even included a chapter with vegan and vegetarian dishes for any non-carnivores reading this book. And in case you didn't read all the little print in the manual that came with your Air Fryer Toaster Oven, I included a chapter outlining everything you need to know about how to use and care for it. Now let's get cooking!

Chapter 1 – Crash Course on Your Air Fryer Toaster Oven

It seems that every other month some new kitchen gadget appears in our stores. Many of them boast that they can simplify your time spent in the kitchen. And many of them achieve that goal. While others turn out to be nothing more than a passing fad. But this new Cuisinart Air Fryer Toaster Oven will make cooking almost any meal easier to do.

The countertop appliance performs a variety of cooking techniques. Most of these are mentioned in the name of the oven. Yes, it will toast and even air fry. But, the oven also has two settings, bake, and convection bake along with broil and convection broil that enhance the quality of the meals you make. Let's take a closer look at these functions.

Inside the Oven

Your toaster oven comes with a wire rack, baking pan, and a fryer basket. Inside the oven, you will see position 1 and position 2 slots. Both the rack and baking pan slide into these slots. What you are cooking and what function you are using determines which position you need to use.

Position 1 is ideal for baking delicate dishes, such as cakes. And for baking large items, like a beef roast or whole chicken. You would also use position 1 for casseroles and loaves of bread.

Position 2 is used for toasting, air frying, warming, and broiling. You can use position 2 when baking some items like cookies, brownies, and pastries which need to cook to a nice, golden brown.

Cooking Functions

Toast – Always use position 2 when toasting. Make sure the items you wanted to be toasted are centered on the rack or baking pan. To toast bread, bagels, English muffins, or other items first set the function dial to Toast. Set the temperature to Toast/Broil then set the on/Toast Timer to the desired setting, from light to dark. The timer will ding when the cycle has ended and the oven will turn off.

Warm – Unlike a microwave, your Cuisinart oven will reheat food evenly. So no more hot and cold spots. You can also use the warm function to reheat fried food and make them crisp again. How big the item is you are warming will determine what rack position to use. For warming foods, set function dial and temperature dial to Warm. Then turn the on/Timer button to the desired length of time you need, like 10 minutes.

Broil/Convection Broil – Broiling is good for meats, melting cheese and toppings on sandwiches, and for browning the tops of casseroles. Convection broil should be used for meats and fish as it browns food on all sides, not just the top. Generally, when broiling, you would use position 2 and the baking pan and fryer basket together. Set the function to either Broil or Convection Broil and temperature dial to Toast/Broil. Then just set the timer for the desired cooking time. Keep an eye on your food as it browns quite quickly on either of these functions.

Bake/Convection Bake – The bake function works just like a traditional oven. This setting is perfect for meats, casseroles, and delicate baked goods like cakes, muffins, and pastry. Convection Bake uses a fan to circulate the heat so food browns evenly and cooks faster. Use Convection Bake for things like pizza, bread, scones, and to roast meats. When convection baking you should reduce the temperature in the recipe by 25 degrees so you don't overcook your food. (You won't need to do that with the recipes in this book though.)

Like the previous function set the function dial to bake or convection bake. Then select the desired temperature. For most baked items, the oven should be preheated first. To do that with the Cuisinart, add five minutes to the desired cooking time. For example, if the recipe says to bake 30 minutes, set the on/Timer dial to 35 minutes. Wait five minutes before putting your dish in the oven.

Air Fry – When air frying foods, the baking pan should always be in position 2. You will place your food items in the fryer basket and set it on the baking pan. The baking pan works as a drip pan. You will notice that there will some space between the basket and the pan, this allows the heat to cook and crisp your food from all angles. Unlike some of the previous settings, you do not need to preheat the oven when on Air Fry, it heats up quickly.

Air frying is great for preparing food with a crispy, crunchy texture. But unlike traditional frying methods, you won't be adding any calories or grease to your foods. Just set the function dial to Air Fry, then select your temperature and set the timer. For a crispier outside, you can spray the food lightly with cooking spray.

Benefits Of The Cuisinart Air Fryer Oven

Saves you time – This compact oven fits nicely on the kitchen counter, taking up very little space. So, you don't need to move it from cupboard to counter every time you want to use it. It also saves you time since food tends to cook faster in this toaster oven than it does in a traditional oven. The Cuisinart oven is larger than the usual air fryer, so you save time by being able to cook larger quantities of food at one time.

Saves you money – The toaster oven uses less electricity than your old oven. This saves you money on monthly bills. It also saves you money since it features so many cooking functions, you won't need a bunch of other kitchen gadgets that clutter up your cupboards.

Saves you from unwanted fat and calories – Traditional fried foods are cooked in oil and grease. But air frying uses hot air that is circulated around the food giving it the same crispy crunch as oil frying. But now you get to eliminate 80% of the fat from your diet which equals a lot fewer calories.

The Secret That Makes This Oven Work

Air frying is accomplished by circulating hot air inside the oven. The Cuisinart air fryer toaster oven has a heavy-duty fan on the top of the unit and inside the oven. So, the hot air reaches every surface of the food you are cooking to create a crispy, golden brown outside. As long as you don't overcook your food, it will be tender and juicy inside. Another feature the Cuisinart has is a fan on the inside that circulates and filters the hot air. This means you won't have any nasty cooking odors, like the smell of onions or fish in your home.

When the oven is set to broil, bake, or toast, it works like any oven, with an overhead heating element that distributes heat over the top of foods. This helps to cook casseroles, bread, and cake perfectly on the inside while giving foods a crusty, golden brown top.

Features & Specifications
- Seven functions – warm, toast, broil, convection broil, bake, convection bake, and air fry.
- Easy to clean external crumb tray.
- Large capacity fits 8x11-inch baking pans and 11-inch pizza wheels
- Two rack positions for cooking flexibility.
- Four dial controls on the front of the oven.
- 60-minute timer with an auto-shutoff feature.
- Separate control for toast so you get just the shade you want.
- Easy-to-clean nonstick interior.
- When operating the oven is very quiet and won't disturb anyone.

Follow These Tips To Keep You And Your Family Safe
Always unplug the oven when you aren't using it.
Never store anything on the top of the oven.
Do not touch top or sides when the oven is on as it gets very hot.
Unplug the oven and let it cool completely before cleaning.
Do not place any part of the oven in water as this could cause an electric shock.
Avoid fires by NOT placing cardboard, paper, plastic, or other items like these in the oven.
Do not use glass baking dishes when toasting or broiling as they can break.
Do not place the oven too close to your gas or electric stove.
Before unplugging the oven, make sure all the control dials are set to off position.
If using foil in the oven, make sure it does not touch the top or sides of the unit as this can cause a fire or an electric shock.

Questions and Answers

Is the air fryer toaster oven dishwasher safe?
No! When washing the rack, baking pan or fryer basket you should hand wash them in warm soapy water and air dry. To clean the inside and outside of the oven, use a mild detergent with a soft cloth or sponge. Never use any abrasive cleaners or steel wool pads as they can damage your oven.

Is it safe to use foil in the oven?
Using foil is not recommended. It can cover the drip tray causing grease to accumulate and catch fire. If you must use foil, cut it to fit the top of your baking pan or bottom of the included baking pan perfectly. Never let the foil touch the top or sides of the oven.

Do I need to preheat the oven?
That depends on which function you are using. For toasting or air frying food, preheating is not necessary. When baking or broiling allow the oven to preheat for at least five minutes before adding any food.

Can I put battered food in my oven?
Yes, you can. Most crunchy fried foods have some sort of batter or coating on them. Just make sure you use the baking pan and fryer basket together. For best results, lightly spray the fryer basket with a little cooking spray to prevent your food from sticking, and losing all that crunchy coating.

Chapter 2 – Breakfast & Brunch

Bacon Ranch Breakfast Bake

Prep time: 10 minutes, cook time: 35 minutes, Serves: 6

7 Ingredients:
- Nonstick cooking spray
- 1 can refrigerated crescent rolls
- 1 ½ lbs. bacon, chop & cook crisp
- 1 ½ cups cheddar cheese, grated
- 6 eggs
- ½ cup milk
- 1 ½ tbsp. dry Ranch dressing mix
- ½ tsp pepper

Instructions
1. Place the rack in the oven in position one. Lightly spray an 8x11-inch baking pan with cooking spray.
2. Unroll crescents and press on the bottom and sides of prepared pan, pressing the seams together.
3. Sprinkle bacon over the bottom then top with cheese.
4. In a medium bowl, whisk together eggs, milk, dressing mix, and pepper until combined. Pour over bacon and cheese.
5. Set to bake at 350°F for 35 minutes. After 5 minutes, place the pan in the oven and bake until the center is set.
6. Let cool slightly before cutting and serving.

Nutrition Facts Per Serving
Calories 706, Total Fat 48g, Saturated Fat 17g, Total Carbs 17g, Net Carbs 16g, Protein 24g, Sugar 4g, Fiber 1g, Sodium 915mg, Potassium 300mg, Phosphorus 349mg

Italian Sausage & Egg Taquitos

Prep time: 15 minutes, cook time: 15 minutes, Serves; 4

6 Ingredients:
- 3 eggs, scrambled
- 6 oz. hot Italian sausage, cooked & crumbled
- ¼ cup sun dried tomatoes, drain & slice thin
- 1 avocado, halved, pitted, peeled & chopped
- 1 cup sharp cheddar cheese, grated
- 12 corn tortillas, softened

Instructions
1. Line the baking pan with parchment paper.
2. In a large bowl, place all ingredients and toss to mix.
3. One at a time, place a tortilla on a cutting board and add some of the filling mixture. Start at one side and roll tortilla over filling. Place seam side down on prepared pan. Repeat with remaining tortillas and filling.
4. Set to air fry at 425°F for 20 minutes. After 5 minutes, place the pan in position 2 of the oven and cook until taquitos are crisp and the cheese has melted. Serve immediately.

Nutrition Facts Per Serving
Calories 682, Total Fat 36g, Saturated Fat 13g, Total Carbs 39g, Net Carbs 31g, Protein 23g, Sugar 2g, Fiber 8g, Sodium 590mg, Potassium 674mg, Phosphorus 532mg

Strawberry Cheesecake Pastries

Prep time: 10 minutes, cook time: 20 minutes, Serves: 6

7 Ingredients:
- 1 sheet puff pastry, thawed
- ¼ cup cream cheese, soft
- 1 tbsp. strawberry jam
- 1 ½ cups strawberries, sliced
- 1 egg
- 1 tbsp. water
- 6 tsp powdered sugar, sifted

Instructions
1. Line the baking pan with parchment paper.
2. Lay the puff pastry on a cutting board and cut into 6 rectangles. Transfer to prepared pan, placing them 1-inch apart.
3. Lightly score the pastry, creating a ½-inch border, do not cut all the way through. Use a fork to prick the center.
4. In a small bowl, combine cream cheese and jam until thoroughly combined. Spoon mixture evenly into centers of the pastry and spread it within the scored area.
5. Top pastries with sliced berries.
6. In a small bowl, whisk together egg and water. Brush edges of pastry with the egg wash.
7. Set to bake at 350°F for 20 minutes. After 5 minutes, place the baking pan in position 1 and bake pastries until golden brown and puffed.
8. Remove from oven and let cool. Dust with powdered sugar before serving.

Nutrition Facts Per Serving
Calories 205, Total Fat 13g, Saturated Fat 4g, Total Carbs 19g, Net Carbs 18g, Protein 3g, Sugar 6g, Fiber 1g, Sodium 107mg, Potassium 97mg, Phosphorus 50mg

Loaded Breakfast Potatoes

Prep time: 10 minutes, cook time: 20 minutes, Serves: 3

8 Ingredients:
- 3 gold potatoes, chopped
- 2 cloves garlic, diced fine
- ¼ tsp salt
- ¼ tsp pepper
- ½ tsp Old Bay seasoning
- 1 tbsp. olive oil
- 2 slices bacon, cook crisp & crumble
- 1 tbsp. maple syrup

Instructions
1. Place the baking pan in position 2 of the oven.
2. In a large bowl, add potatoes, garlic, and seasonings, toss to combine.
3. Drizzle oil over mixture and toss to coat.
4. Place potatoes in an even layer in the fryer basket and place on the baking pan.
5. Set oven to air fry at 400°F for 15 minutes. Cook until potatoes are nicely browned on the outside, and soft on the inside. Stir halfway through cooking time.
6. Pour potatoes onto the baking pan, sprinkle with bacon and drizzle with syrup.
7. Place the pan in position 2 and set to broil at 400°F. Cook 1-2 minutes to caramelize the potatoes. Serve immediately.

Nutrition Facts Per Serving
Calories 528, Total Fat 24g, Saturated Fat 7g, Total Carbs 70g, Net Carbs 62g, Protein 8g, Sugar 7g, Fiber 8g, Sodium 222mg, Potassium 1582mg, Phosphorus 216mg

Pigs in a Blanket

Prep time: 25 minutes, cook time: 25 minutes, Serves: 6

5 Ingredients:
- 12 breakfast sausage links, cooked
- 6 eggs, scrambled
- ½ cup sharp cheddar cheese, grated
- ¾ cup Southwest hash browns, thawed
- 2 tubes French bread loaf, refrigerated

Instructions
1. Spray the baking pan with cooking spray.
2. Open up can of bread loaf. Divide the dough in half.
3. On a lightly floured surface, roll one half into a 5x12-inch rectangle.
4. Place 3 sausage links along the dough, leaving room in between. Cut dough into 3 equal pieces.
5. Top each sausage with a tablespoon of hash browns, tablespoon of egg, and a sprinkling of cheese. Roll up and seal the edges. Place seam side down on prepared pan. Repeat with remaining dough and filling ingredients.
6. Set oven to convection bake at 325°F for 30 minutes. After 5 minutes, place the pan in position 1 of the oven. Bake for 25 minutes, or until bread is golden brown and cooked through.
7. Let cool on wire rack 5 minutes before serving.

Nutrition Facts Per Serving
Calories 718, Total Fat 14g, Saturated Fat 5g, Total Carbs 74g, Net Carbs 71g, Protein 24g, Sugar 7g, Fiber 3g, Sodium 1115mg, Potassium 321mg, Phosphorus 261mg

Apple Fritter Loaf

Prep time: 15 minutes, cook time: 1 hour, Serves: 10

13 Ingredients:
- Butter flavored cooking spray
- 1/3 cup brown sugar, packed
- 1 tsp. cinnamon, divided
- 1 ½ cups apples, chopped
- 2/3 cup + 1 tsp. sugar, divided
- ½ cup + ½ tbsp. butter, soft, divided
- 2 eggs
- 2 ¼ tsp. vanilla, divided
- 1 ½ cups flour
- 2 tsp baking powder
- ¼ tsp salt
- ½ cup + 2 tbsp. milk
- 1/2 cup powdered sugar

Instructions

1. Place rack in position 1 of the oven. Spray an 8-inch loaf pan with cooking spray.
2. In a small bowl, combine brown sugar and ½ teaspoon cinnamon.
3. Place apples in a medium bowl and sprinkle with remaining cinnamon and 1 teaspoon sugar, toss to coat.
4. In a large bowl, beat remaining sugar and butter until smooth.
5. Beat in eggs and 2 teaspoons vanilla until combined. Stir in flour, baking powder, and salt until combined.
6. Add ½ cup milk and beat until smooth. Pour half the batter in the prepared pan. Add half the apples then remaining batter. Add the remaining apples over the top, pressing lightly. Sprinkle brown sugar mixture over the apples.
7. Set oven to convection bake at 325°F for 5 minutes. Once timer goes, off place bread on the rack and set timer to 1 hour. Bread is done when it passes the toothpick test.
8. Let cool in pan 10 minutes, then invert onto wire rack to cool.
9. In a small bowl, whisk together powdered sugar and butter until smooth. Whisk in remaining milk and vanilla and drizzle over cooled bread.

Nutrition Facts Per Serving

Calories 418, Total Fat 14g, Saturated Fat 8g, Total Carbs 44g, Net Carbs 43g, Protein 4g, Sugar 28g, Fiber 1g, Sodium 85mg, Potassium 190mg, Phosphorus 128mg

Enchiladas 4 Breakfast

Prep time: 20 minutes, cook time: 30 minutes, Serves: 8

15 Ingredients:
- Nonstick cooking spray
- 1 lb. pork breakfast sausage
- 2 cups hash browns, thawed
- 1/3 cup red bell pepper, chopped
- 1/3 cup poblano pepper, chopped
- 6 green onion, sliced thin
- 2 tsp garlic salt divided
- 10 eggs
- 1 tsp black pepper
- 3 cups pepper jack cheese, grated
- 8 8-inch
- 1 cup salsa Verde
- ½ cup half & half
- ½ tsp cumin
- ½ tsp oregano

Instructions

1. Place the rack in position 1. Lightly spray an 8x11-inch baking dish with cooking spray.
2. In a medium saucepan, over medium heat, cook sausage until no longer pink. Use a slotted spoon to transfer to a paper towel lined plate.
3. Add potatoes, red pepper, poblano, 1 teaspoon garlic salt, and onion (saving 3 tablespoons for garnish) to the pan. Cook until vegetables are fork-tender, about 5-7 minutes. Stir in sausage and stir to combine. Remove from heat.
4. In a medium bowl, whisk eggs, remaining garlic salt, and pepper.
5. Heat a medium skillet over medium heat. Once hot, add eggs and scramble until done. Remove from heat.
6. Place tortillas, one at a time, on work surface. Use 2 cups of cheese for filling. Sprinkle some cheese down the middle. Top with sausage mixture and a little more cheese. Roll up and place seam side down in prepared pan. Repeat with remaining ingredients.
7. In a small bowl, whisk together salsa Verde, half & half, cumin, and oregano. Pour over enchiladas and top with remaining cheese.
8. Set to bake on 375°F for 35 minutes. After 5 minutes, place baking pan on rack and bake 30 minutes or until golden brown and bubbly. Serve garnished with reserved onions.

Nutrition Facts Per Serving
Calories 582, Total Fat 36g, Saturated Fat 15g, Total Carbs 31g, Net Carbs 28g, Protein 31g, Sugar 4g, Fiber 3g, Sodium 1015mg, Potassium 677mg, Phosphorus 512mg

Cinnamon Streusel Bread

Prep time: 1 hour, cook time: 30 minutes, Serves: 8

11 Ingredients:
- 1 cup warm water
- 1 envelope yeast, quick rising
- 1/3 cup + 6 tsp milk, divided
- 1 egg
- 3 tbsp. sugar
- 3 ½ cups flour, divided
- 1 tbsp. + 2 tsp olive oil
- 1 tsp salt
- 2 tbsp. cinnamon
- ½ cup brown sugar
- 2 tbsp. butter, cold & cut in cubes
- 1 cup powdered sugar

Instructions
1. In a large bowl, add water and sprinkle yeast over top, stir to dissolve.
2. Stir in 1/3 cup milk, egg, and sugar until combined.
3. Add 2 cups flour and stir in until batter gets thick. With a wooden spoon, or mixer with dough hook attached, beat 100 strokes.
4. Fold in oil and salt. Then stir in 1 ¼ cups flour until dough begins to come together.
5. Mix in cinnamon and transfer dough to a lightly floured work surface. Knead for 5 minutes then form into a ball.
6. Use remaining oil to grease a clean bowl and add dough. Cover and let rise 30 minutes.
7. Spray a 9-inch loaf pan with cooking spray.
8. After 30 minutes, punch dough down and divide into 8 equal pieces.
9. Place brown sugar in a shallow bowl and roll dough pieces in it, forming it into balls. Place in prepared pan and sprinkle remaining brown sugar over top.
10. In a small bowl, combine butter and ¼ cup flour until mixture resembles coarse crumbs. Sprinkle over top of bread.
11. Place rack in position 1 of the oven. Set to convection bake on 325°F and set timer for 35 minutes. After 5 minutes, add pan to the rack and bake 30 minutes or until golden brown.
12. Let cool in pan 10 minutes, then invert onto wire rack.
13. In a small bowl, whisk together powdered sugar and milk until smooth. Drizzle over warm bread and serve.

Nutrition Facts Per Serving
Calories 328, Total Fat 6g, Saturated Fat 2g, Total Carbs 60g, Net Carbs 58g, Protein 6g, Sugar 25g, Fiber 2g, Sodium 266mg, Potassium 94mg, Phosphorus 71mg

Brioche Breakfast Pudding

Prep time: 10 minutes, cook time: 45 minutes, Serves: 8

10 Ingredients:
- 1 loaf brioche bread, cut in cubes
- ½ tbsp. coconut oil, soft
- 4 cups milk
- 1 can coconut milk
- 6 eggs
- ½ cup sugar
- 2 tsp vanilla
- ¼ tsp salt
- 1 cup coconut, shredded
- ½ cup chocolate chips

Instructions

1. Place rack in position 1 of the oven. Grease an 8x11-inch baking pan with coconut oil.
2. Add the bread cubes to the pan, pressing lightly to settle.
3. In a large bowl, whisk together milk, coconut milk, eggs, sugar, vanilla, and salt until combined.
4. Stir in coconut and chocolate chips. Pour evenly over bread. Cover with plastic wrap and refrigerate 2 hours or overnight.
5. Set oven to bake on 350°F for 50 minutes. After 5 minutes, add the pudding to the oven and bake 40-45 minutes, or until top is beginning to brown and it passes the toothpick test.
6. Remove to wire rack and let cool 5-10 minutes before serving.

Nutrition Facts Per Serving

Calories 476, Total Fat 24g, Saturated Fat 15g, Total Carbs 51g, Net Carbs 48g, Protein 14g, Sugar 30g, Fiber 3g, Sodium 398mg, Potassium 443mg, Phosphorus 288mg

Strawberry Basil Muffins

Prep time: 15 minutes, cook time: 20 minutes, Serves: 12

13 Ingredients:
- 3 tbsp. almonds
- ¾ cup + 2 tbsp. flour, divided
- ½ cup + 2 tbsp. brown sugar, divided
- ½ tsp salt, divided
- ¼ cup + 2 tbsp. coconut oil, melted
- 1 cup white whole-wheat flour
- 2 tsp baking powder
- 1 tsp baking soda
- 1 ¼ cup buttermilk, low fat
- 1 egg
- 1 tsp vanilla
- 1 ½ cups strawberries, chopped
- ¼ cup fresh basil, chopped

Instructions

1. Place rack in position 1 of the oven. Line 2 6-cup muffin tins with paper liners.
2. Place almonds, 2 tablespoons flour, 2 tablespoons brown sugar, and ¼ teaspoon salt in the food processor or blender. Pulse until finely ground. Transfer to a small bowl and stir in 2 tablespoons oil until combined.
3. In a large bowl, combine remaining flour, whole wheat flour, baking powder, baking soda, and remaining salt together.
4. In a separate large bowl, whisk together, remaining brown sugar, oil, buttermilk, juice, egg and vanilla until thoroughly combined.
5. Make a well in the dry ingredients and add wet ingredients, stir just until combined.
6. Fold in berries and basil. Divide evenly between prepared pans. Sprinkle almond topping over muffins.
7. Set oven to bake on 400°F for 25 minutes. After 5 minutes, add muffin tins, one at a time, to oven and bake 18-20 minutes or until muffins pass the toothpick test. Let cool in pan 10 minutes, then transfer to wire rack to cool completely.

Nutrition Facts Per Serving

Calories 209, Total Fat 7g, Saturated Fat 6g, Total Carbs 30g, Net Carbs 28g, Protein 4g, Sugar 14g, Fiber 2g, Sodium 239mg, Potassium 231mg, Phosphorus 140mg

Chapter 3 – Fish & Seafood

Salmon Burgers

Prep time: 10 minutes, cook time: 10 minutes, Serves: 4

7 Ingredients:
- 14.75 oz. can salmon, drain & flake
- ¼ cup onion, chopped fine
- 1 egg
- ¼ cup multi-grain crackers, crushed
- 2 tsp fresh dill, chopped
- ¼ tsp pepper
- Nonstick cooking spray

Instructions
1. In a medium bowl, combine all ingredients until combined. Form into 4 patties.
2. Lightly spray fryer basket with cooking spray. Place the baking pan in position 2 of the oven.
3. Set oven to air fryer on 350°F.
4. Place the patties in the basket and set on baking pan. Set timer for 8 minutes. Cook until burgers are golden brown, turning over halfway through cooking time. Serve on toasted buns with choice of toppings.

Nutrition Facts Per Serving
Calories 330, Total Fat 10g, Saturated Fat 2g, Total Carbs 11g, Net Carbs 11g, Protein 24g, Sugar 0g, Fiber 0g, Sodium 643mg, Potassium 407mg, Phosphorus 391mg

Air Fried Haddock Filets

Prep time: 10 minutes, cook time: 20 minutes, Serves: 8

6 Ingredients:
- Nonstick cooking spray
- 2 egg whites
- ½ tsp dill
- ½ tsp pepper
- 1 cup cornflakes, crushed
- 2 lbs. haddock fillets, cut in 8 pieces

Instructions
1. Place baking pan in position 2 of the oven. Lightly spray fryer basket with cooking spray.
2. In a shallow bowl, whisk together egg whites, dill, and pepper.
3. Place crushed cornflakes in a separate shallow dish.
4. Dip fish in egg mixture, then cornflakes, coating completely. Place in fryer basket.
5. Place basket on the baking pan and set oven to air fryer on 400°F. Cook 18-20 minutes, turning over halfway through, until fish flakes easily with a fork. Serve.

Nutrition Facts Per Serving
Calories 193, Total Fat 1g, Saturated Fat 0g, Total Carbs 7g, Net Carbs 7g, Protein 39g, Sugar 1g, Fiber 0g, Sodium 568mg, Potassium 692mg, Phosphorus 524mg

Crispy Coated Scallops

Prep time: 10 minutes, cook time: 10 minutes, Serves: 4

9 Ingredients:
- Nonstick cooking spray
- 1 lb. sea scallops, patted dry
- 1 teaspoon onion powder
- ½ tsp pepper
- 1 egg
- 1 tbsp. water
- ¼ cup Italian bread crumbs
- Paprika
- 1 tbsp. fresh lemon juice

Instructions

1. Lightly spray fryer basket with cooking spray. Place baking pan in position 2 of the oven.
2. Sprinkle scallops with onion powder and pepper.
3. In a shallow dish, whisk together egg and water.
4. Place bread crumbs in a separate shallow dish.
5. Dip scallops in egg then bread crumbs coating them lightly. Place in fryer basket and lightly spray with cooking spray. Sprinkle with paprika.
6. Place the basket on the baking pan and set oven to air fryer on 400°F. Bake 10-12 minutes until scallops are firm on the inside and golden brown on the outside. Drizzle with lemon juice and serve.

Nutrition Facts Per Serving

Calories 122, Total Fat 2g, Saturated Fat 1g, Total Carbs 10g, Net Carbs 9g, Protein 16g, Sugar 1g, Fiber 1g, Sodium 563mg, Potassium 282mg, Phosphorus 420mg

Tasty Tuna Loaf

Prep time: 10 minutes, cook time: 40 minutes, Serves: 6

11 Ingredients:
- Nonstick cooking spray
- 12 oz. can chunk white tuna in water, drain & flake
- ¾ cup bread crumbs
- 1 onion, chopped fine
- 2 eggs, beaten
- ¼ cup milk
- ½ tsp fresh lemon juice
- ½ tsp dill
- 1 tbsp. fresh parsley, chopped
- ½ tsp salt
- ½ tsp pepper

Instructions

1. Place rack in position 1 of the oven. Spray a 9-inch loaf pan with cooking spray.
2. In a large bowl, combine all ingredients until thoroughly mixed. Spread evenly in prepared pan.
3. Set oven to bake on 350°F for 45 minutes. After 5 minutes, place the pan in the oven and cook 40 minutes, or until top is golden brown. Slice and serve.

Nutrition Facts Per Serving

Calories 169, Total Fat 5g, Saturated Fat 1g, Total Carbs 13g, Net Carbs 12g, Protein 18g, Sugar 3g, Fiber 1g, Sodium 540mg, Potassium 247mg, Phosphorus 202mg

Maryland Crab Cakes

Prep time: 10 minutes, cook time: 10 minutes, Serves: 6

11 Ingredients:
- Nonstick cooking spray
- 2 eggs
- 1 cup Panko bread crumbs
- 1 stalk celery, chopped
- 3 tbsp. mayonnaise
- 1 tsp Worcestershire sauce
- ¼ cup mozzarella cheese, grated
- 1 tsp Italian seasoning
- 1 tbsp. fresh parsley, chopped
- 1 tsp pepper
- ¾ lb. lump crabmeat, drained

Instructions
1. Place baking pan in position 2 of the oven. Lightly spray the fryer basket with cooking spray.
2. In a large bowl, combine all ingredients except crab meat, mix well.
3. Fold in crab carefully so it retains some chunks. Form mixture into 12 patties.
4. Place patties in a single layer in the fryer basket. Place the basket on the baking pan.
5. Set oven to air fryer on 350°F for 10 minutes. Cook until golden brown, turning over halfway through cooking time. Serve immediately.

Nutrition Facts Per Serving

Calories 172, Total Fat 8g, Saturated Fat 2g, Total Carbs 14g, Net Carbs 13g, Protein 16g, Sugar 1g, Fiber 1g, Sodium 527mg, Potassium 290mg, Phosphorus 201mg

Mediterranean Sole

Prep time: 15 minutes, cook time: 20 minutes, Serves: 6

11 Ingredients:
- Nonstick cooking spray
- 2 tbsp. olive oil
- 8 scallions, sliced thin
- 2 cloves garlic, diced fine
- 4 tomatoes, chopped
- ½ cup dry white wine
- 2 tbsp. fresh parsley, chopped fine
- 1 tsp oregano
- 1 tsp pepper
- 2 lbs. sole, cut in 6 pieces
- 4 oz. feta cheese, crumbled

Instructions

1. Place the rack in position 1 of the oven. Spray an 8x11-inch baking dish with cooking spray.
2. Heat the oil in a medium skillet over medium heat. Add scallions and garlic and cook until tender, stirring frequently.
3. Add the tomatoes, wine, parsley, oregano, and pepper. Stir to mix. Simmer for 5 minutes, or until sauce thickens. Remove from heat.
4. Pour half the sauce on the bottom of the prepared dish. Lay fish on top then pour remaining sauce over the top. Sprinkle with feta.
5. Set the oven to bake on 400°F for 25 minutes. After 5 minutes, place the baking dish on the rack and cook 15-18 minutes or until fish flakes easily with a fork. Serve immediately.

Nutrition Facts Per Serving

Calories 220, Total Fat 12g, Saturated Fat 4g, Total Carbs 6g, Net Carbs 4g, Protein 22g, Sugar 4g, Fiber 2g, Sodium 631mg, Potassium 540mg, Phosphorus 478mg

Coconut Shrimp

Prep time: 15 minutes, cook time: 10 minutes, Serves: 6

9 Ingredients:
- Nonstick cooking spray
- 1/3 cup cornstarch
- ½ tsp cayenne pepper
- 1/8 tsp salt
- 2 egg whites
- 1 tbsp. honey
- 1 tbsp. fresh lime juice
- ½ cup sweetened coconut, chopped fine
- 1 ½ lbs. large shrimp, peel, devein & leave tails on

Instructions
1. Place the baking pan in position 2 of the oven. Lightly spray the fryer basket with cooking spray.
2. In a small bowl, combine cornstarch, cayenne pepper, and salt.
3. In a separate small bowl, whisk together egg whites, honey, and lime juice.
4. Place the coconut in a shallow dish.
5. Dredge shrimp in the cornstarch mixture, then egg and finally roll in coconut to coat. Place in a single layer in the basket. Spray lightly with cooking spray.
6. Place basket on the baking pan and set oven to air fry on 425°F for 10 minutes. Cook until shrimp are pink and coconut is lightly toasted. Serve immediately.

Nutrition Facts Per Serving
Calories 136, Total Fat 3g, Saturated Fat 2g, Total Carbs 14g, Net Carbs 13g, Protein 17g, Sugar 6g, Fiber 1g, Sodium 733mg, Potassium 180mg, Phosphorus 287mg

Spicy Grilled Halibut

Prep time: 30 minutes, cook time: 10 minutes, Serves: 4

5 Ingredients:
- ½ cup fresh lemon juice
- 2 jalapeno peppers, seeded & chopped fine
- 4 6 oz. halibut fillets
- Nonstick cooking spray
- ¼ cup cilantro, chopped

Instructions
1. In a small bowl, combine lemon juice and chilies, mix well.
2. Place fish in a large Ziploc bag and add marinade. Toss to coat. Refrigerate 30 minutes.
3. Lightly spray the baking pan with cooking spray. Set oven to broil on 400°F for 15 minutes.
4. After 5 minutes, lay fish on the pan and place in position 2 of the oven. Cook 10 minutes, or until fish flakes easily with a fork. Turn fish over and brush with marinade halfway through cooking time.
5. Sprinkle with cilantro before serving.

Nutrition Facts Per Serving
Calories 328, Total Fat 24g, Saturated Fat 4g, Total Carbs 3g, Net Carbs 3g, Protein 25g, Sugar 1g, Fiber 0g, Sodium 137mg, Potassium 510mg, Phosphorus 284mg

Tropical Shrimp Skewers

Prep time: 15 minutes, cook time: 5 minutes, Serves: 4
10 Ingredients:
- 1 tbsp. lime juice
- 1 tbsp. honey
- ¼ tsp red pepper flakes
- ¼ tsp pepper
- ¼ tsp ginger
- Nonstick cooking spray
- 1 lb. medium shrimp, peel, devein & leave tails on
- 2 cups peaches, drain & chop
- ½ green bell pepper, chopped fine
- ¼ cup scallions, chopped

Instructions
1. Soak 8 small wooden skewers in water for 15 minutes.
2. In a small bowl, whisk together lime juice, honey and spices. Transfer 2 tablespoons of the mixture to a medium bowl.
3. Place the baking pan in position 2 of the oven. Lightly spray fryer basket with cooking spray. Set oven to broil on 400°F for 10 minutes.
4. Thread 5 shrimp on each skewer and brush both sides with marinade. Place in basket and after 5 minutes, place on the baking pan. Cook 4-5 minutes or until shrimp turn pink.
5. Add peaches, bell pepper, and scallions to reserved honey mixture, mix well. Divide salsa evenly between serving plates and top with 2 skewers each. Serve immediately.

Nutrition Facts Per Serving
Calories 181, Total Fat 1g, Saturated Fat 0g, Total Carbs 27g, Net Carbs 25g, Protein 16g, Sugar 21g, Fiber 2g, Sodium 650mg, Potassium 288mg, Phosphorus 297mg

Seafood Mac n Cheese

Prep time: 20 minutes, cook time: 30 minutes, Serves: 8

16 Ingredients:
- Nonstick cooking spray
- 16 oz. macaroni
- 7 tbsp. butter, divided
- ¾ lb. medium shrimp, peel, devein, & cut in ½-inch pieces
- ½ cup Italian panko bread crumbs
- 1 cup onion, chopped fine
- 1 ½ tsp garlic, diced fine
- 1/3 cup flour
- 3 cups milk
- 1/8 tsp nutmeg
- ½ tsp Old Bay seasoning
- 1 tsp salt
- ¾ tsp pepper
- 1 1/3 cup Parmesan cheese, grated
- 1 1/3 cup Swiss cheese, grated
- 1 1/3 cup sharp cheddar cheese, grated
- ½ lb. lump crab meat, cooked

Instructions
1. Place wire rack in position 1 of the oven. Spray a 7x11-inch baking dish with cooking spray.
2. Cook macaroni according to package directions, shortening cooking time by 2 minutes. Drain and rinse with cold water.
3. Melt 1 tablespoon butter in a large skillet over med-high heat. Add shrimp and cook, stirring, until they turn pink. Remove from heat.
4. Melt remaining butter in a large saucepan over medium heat. Once melted, transfer 2 tablespoons to a small bowl and mix in bread crumbs.
5. Add onions and garlic to saucepan and cook, stirring, until they soften.
6. Whisk in flour and cook 1 minute, until smooth.
7. Whisk in milk until there are no lumps. Bring to a boil, reduce heat and simmer until thickened, whisking constantly.
8. Whisk in seasonings. Stir in cheese until melted and smooth. Fold in macaroni and seafood. Transfer to prepared dish. Sprinkle bread crumb mixture evenly over top.
9. Set oven to bake on 400°F for 25 minutes. After 5 minutes, place dish on the rack and bake 20 minutes, until topping is golden brown and sauce is bubbly. Let cool 5 minutes before serving.

Nutrition Facts Per Serving
Calories 672, Total Fat 26g, Saturated Fat 15g, Total Carbs 68g, Net Carbs 61g, Protein 39g, Sugar 7g, Fiber 7g, Sodium 996mg, Potassium 921mg, Phosphorus 714mg

Chapter 4 – Beef, Lamb & Pork

Pork Wellington

Prep time: 20 minutes, cook time: 30 minutes, Serves: 6

12 Ingredients:
- 1 ½ lb. pork tenderloin
- ½ tsp salt
- ½ tsp pepper
- 1 tsp thyme
- 1 sheet puff pastry
- 4 oz. prosciutto, sliced thin
- 1 tbsp. Dijon mustard
- 1 tbsp. olive oil
- 1 tbsp. butter
- 8 oz. mushrooms, chopped
- 1 shallot, chopped
- 1 egg, beaten

Instructions
1. Season tenderloin with salt, pepper, and thyme on all sides.
2. On parchment covered work surface, roll out pastry as long as the tenderloin and wide enough to cover it completely.
3. Lay the prosciutto across the pastry to cover it and spread with mustard.
4. Melt butter and oil in a large skillet over high heat. Add mushrooms and shallot and cook 5-10 minutes, until golden brown. Remove from pan.
5. Add tenderloin to the skillet and brown on all sides.
6. Spread mushrooms over mustard and add pork. Roll up to completely cover tenderloin. Use beaten egg to seal the edge.
7. Set oven to bake on 425°F for 35 minutes.
8. Line baking pan with parchment paper and place pork on it, seam side down. Brush top with remaining egg. After oven preheats 5 minutes, place pan in position 1 and cook 30 or until puffed and golden brown.
9. Remove from oven and let rest 5 minutes before slicing and serving.

Nutrition Facts Per Serving
Calories 457, Total Fat 25g, Saturated Fat 7g, Total Carbs 20g, Net Carbs 19g, Protein 38g, Sugar 1g, Fiber 1g, Sodium 627mg, Potassium 706mg, Phosphorus 409mg

Garlic Infused Roast Beef

Prep time: 10 minutes, cook time: 75 minutes, Serves: 10

7 Ingredients:
- 3 lb. beef roast, room temperature
- 4 cloves garlic, cut in thin slivers
- Olive oil spray,
- 1 tsp salt
- 1 tsp pepper
- 2 tsp rosemary

Instructions

1. Trim off the fat from the roast. Use a sharp knife to pierce the roast in intervals, ½-inch deep. Insert garlic sliver in holes, pushing into the meat.
2. Lightly spray the beef with oil and season with salt, pepper, and rosemary.
3. Place the baking pan in position 1 of the oven. Set to convection bake on 325°F for 60 minutes.
4. Spray the fryer basket with oil and place roast in it. Once the oven has preheated for 5 minutes, place the basket on the pan. Cook 60 minutes, or until beef reaches desired doneness.
5. Remove from oven and let rest 10 minutes. Slice thinly and serve.

Nutrition Facts Per Serving

Calories 265, Total Fat 13g, Saturated Fat 5g, Total Carbs 1g, Net Carbs 1g, Protein 36g, Sugar 0g, Fiber 0g, Sodium 342mg, Potassium 478mg, Phosphorus 288mg

Stuffed Pork Loin

Prep time: 25 minutes, cook time: 35 minutes, Serves: 8

10 Ingredients:
- 3 tbsp. butter
- 2 onions, sliced thin
- ½ cup beef broth
- 3 lb. pork loin, center cut
- 2 tbsp. extra virgin olive oil
- 1 tsp salt
- 1/4 tsp pepper
- 1 tsp Italian seasoning
- 2 cups gruyere cheese, grated
- Nonstick cooking spray

Instructions
1. Melt butter in a large skillet over med-high heat. Add onions and broth and cook until onions are brown and tender, about 15 minutes. Transfer to bowl and keep warm.
2. Butterfly the pork making sure you do not cut all the way through. Open up the tenderloin, cover with plastic wrap and pound to 1/3-inch thick.
3. In a small bowl, combine salt, pepper, and Italian seasoning. Rub both sides of pork with mixture.
4. Spread half the cooked onions on one side of pork and top with half the cheese. Tightly roll up pork and tie with butcher string.
5. Heat oil in skillet. Add the tenderloin and brown on all sides.
6. Set the oven to convection bake on 425°F for 35 minutes.
7. Lightly spray the baking pan with cooking spray and place pork on it. After the oven has preheated for 5 minutes, place the baking pan in position 1 and cook 30 minutes. Basting occasionally with juice from the pan.
8. Top pork with remaining onions and cheese. Increase heat to broil and cook another 5 minutes, or until cheese is melted and golden brown. Let rest 5 minutes before slicing and serving.

Nutrition Facts Per Serving
Calories 448, Total Fat 24g, Saturated Fat 11g, Total Carbs 3g, Net Carbs 0g, Protein 55g, Sugar 1g, Fiber 0g, Sodium 715mg, Potassium 795mg, Phosphorus 665mg

Beef Chimichangas

Prep time: 20 minutes, cook time: 10 minutes, Serves: 4

8 Ingredients:
- 1 lb. ground beef
- 1 tbsp. taco seasoning
- 1/3 cup salsa
- 4 flour tortillas
- 16 oz. refried beans
- 1 cup Mexican cheese blend, grated
- 1 cup lettuce, shredded
- 1 tbsp. olive oil

Instructions
1. Heat a medium skillet over medium heat. Add beef and taco seasoning and cook, breaking up with spatula, until meat is no longer pink. Stir in salsa and remove from heat.
2. Place tortillas, one at a time, on work surface and spread with 1/3 cup beans, leaving a 1-inch border.
3. Top with beef mixture, cheese and lettuce. Fold one edge of the tortilla to the middle, then the opposite edge so they overlap slightly. Fold other two ends towards middle until you have a rectangular pocket.
4. Place the baking pan in position 2 of the oven. Lightly brush Chimichangas with oil and place in fryer basket. Place on baking pan.
5. Set oven to air fry on 400°F for 10 minutes. Cook until Chimichangas are golden brown and crispy. Serve immediately with your favorite toppings.

Nutrition Facts Per Serving
Calories 638, Total Fat 22g, Saturated Fat 9g, Total Carbs 58g, Net Carbs 42g, Protein 52g, Sugar 3g, Fiber 12g, Sodium 928mg, Potassium 1045mg, Phosphorus 650mg

Chinese BBQ Pork

Prep time: 10 minutes, cook time: 40 minutes, Serves: 8

6 Ingredients:
- ½ cup soy sauce
- 2 tbsp. hoisin sauce
- ½ tsp Chinese five spice
- 1 tsp Sriracha sauce
- 1 cup brown sugar
- 3 lbs. pork shoulder, boneless, cut in 2-3-inch cubes

Instructions

1. In a large bowl, whisk together soy sauce, hoisin, five spice, Sriracha, and sugar until sugar is almost dissolved.
2. Add pork and toss to coat well. Cover and refrigerate overnight, stir occasionally.
3. Place baking pan in position 1 of the oven. Set to convection bake on 325°F for 45 minutes.
4. Add the pork to the fryer basket in a single layer. After oven has preheated for 5 minutes, place basket on baking pan. Cook 40 minutes, or until pork is cooked through, flipping over halfway through cooking time. Use marinade to baste meat occasionally. Serve immediately.

Nutrition Facts Per Serving

Calories 344, Total Fat 6g, Saturated Fat 2g, Total Carbs 30g, Net Carbs 30g, Protein 40g, Sugar 28g, Fiber 0g, Sodium 754mg, Potassium 743mg, Phosphorus 319mg

Tender Baby Back Ribs

Prep time: 5 minutes, cook time: 45 minutes, Serves: 4

12 Ingredients:
- 1 rack baby back ribs, separated in 2-3 rib sections
- 1 tsp salt
- 1 tsp pepper
- 2 cloves garlic, crushed
- 1 bay leaf
- 3 tbsp. white wine
- 2 tbsp. olive oil
- 1 tsp lemon juice
- ¼ tsp paprika
- 1 tsp soy sauce
- 2 thyme stems
- Nonstick cooking spray

Instructions
1. In a large bowl, combine all ingredients, except ribs, and mix well.
2. Add ribs and turn to coat all sides. Let marinate at room temperature 30 minutes.
3. Lightly spray fryer basket with cooking spray. Place baking pan in position 1 of the oven.
4. Add ribs to basket, in a single layer, and place on baking pan. Set oven to air fry on 360°F for 45 minutes. Baste ribs with marinade and turn a few times while cooking. Serve immediately.

Nutrition Facts Per Serving
Calories 772, Total Fat 52g, Saturated Fat 10g, Total Carbs 2g, Net Carbs 2g, Protein 74g, Sugar 0g, Fiber 0g, Sodium 864mg, Potassium 1255mg, Phosphorus 749mg

Crispy Lamb Chops

Prep time: 10 minutes, cook time: 15 minutes, Serves: 5

7 Ingredients:
- 10 lamb chop cutlets, bone in & fat removed
- 1 cup bread crumbs
- 1 tbsp. parmesan cheese, grated
- 2 eggs
- ¼ tsp salt
- ¼ tsp pepper
- Nonstick cooking spray

Instructions
1. In a shallow dish, combine breadcrumbs and parmesan.
2. In a separate shallow dish, whisk eggs with salt and pepper.
3. Place baking pan in position 2 of the oven. Lightly spray fryer basket with cooking spray.
4. Dip chops first in egg mixture then in breadcrumbs to coat both sides. Place in single layer in the basket, these will need to be cooked in batches.
5. Place basket on the baking pan and set oven to air fry on 350°F for 6 minutes. Cook chops turning them over halfway through cooking time. Repeat with remaining chops and serve.

Nutrition Facts Per Serving
Calories 233, Total Fat 9g, Saturated Fat 3g, Total Carbs 16g, Net Carbs 15g, Protein 22g, Sugar 1g, Fiber 1g, Sodium 386mg, Potassium 348mg, Phosphorus 240mg

Garlic Butter Pork Chops

Prep time: 5 minutes, cook time: 10 minutes, Serves: 4
7 Ingredients:
- 4 pork chops, boneless
- ½ tsp salt
- ¼ tsp pepper
- 1 tbsp. olive oil
- 4 tbsp. butter
- 1 tsp thyme
- 5 cloves garlic, diced fine

Instructions
1. Sprinkle both sides of chops with salt and pepper.
2. Place baking pan in position 2 of the oven. Set to broil on 400°F for 15 minutes.
3. Heat oil and butter in a small skillet on med-high heat. Add thyme and garlic and cook, stirring 2 minutes, or until garlic starts to brown.
4. After the oven has preheated for 5 minutes, place chops on the baking pan and cover with garlic butter mixture. Cook 10 minutes, or until chops are cooked through, turning them over halfway through and basting with butter sauce. Serve immediately.

Nutrition Facts Per Serving
Calories 415, Total Fat 23g, Saturated Fat 10g, Total Carbs 1g, Net Carbs 1g, Protein 51g, Sugar 0g, Fiber 0g, Sodium 494mg, Potassium 900mg, Phosphorus 540mg

Honey BBQ Lamb Chops

Prep time: 5 minutes, cook time: 10 minutes, Serves: 6

6 Ingredients:
- Nonstick cooking spray
- 2 tbsp. tomato sauce
- 2 tbsp. honey
- 1 tsp garlic, crushed
- 1 tsp green chili, diced fine
- 12 lamb loin chops or cutlets

Instructions
1. Place baking pan in position 2 of the oven. Lightly spray the fryer basket with cooking spray.
2. In a small bowl, whisk together tomato sauce, honey, garlic, and green chili.
3. Heat the oven to broil on 400°F for 15 minutes.
4. Brush both sides of lamb with sauce. Place in a single layer in the basket, you will need to cook them in batches.
5. After the oven preheats for 5 minutes, place basket on the baking pan. Cook 6-7 minutes, turning chops over halfway through cooking time. Serve immediately.

Nutrition Facts Per Serving
Calories 372, Total Fat 6g, Saturated Fat 2g, Total Carbs 6g, Net Carbs 6g, Protein 17g, Sugar 6g, Fiber 0g, Sodium 91mg, Potassium 296mg, Phosphorus 161mg

Country Fried Steak

Prep time: 10 minutes, cook time: 15 minutes, Serves: 4

10 Ingredients:
- 1 egg
- ½ cup flour
- ½ tsp garlic powder
- ½ tsp onion powder
- ½ tsp paprika
- ½ tbsp. cayenne pepper
- 1 lb. round steak, cut in 4 pieces
- ½ tsp salt
- ¼ tsp pepper
- Nonstick cooking spray

Instructions
1. In a shallow dish, beat the egg.
2. In a separate shallow dish, combine flour, garlic powder, onion powder, paprika, and cayenne pepper.
3. Place steaks between plastic wrap and pound to flatten slightly. Sprinkle both sides of the steak with salt and pepper.
4. Dip steak in egg then sprinkle flour mixture over. Repeat. Spray one side of steaks with cooking spray.
5. Place baking pan in position 2 of the oven. Place steaks, sprayed side down, in fryer basket and spray the top side.
6. Place the basket on the baking pan and set oven to air fry on 360°F for 10 minutes.
7. Turn steaks over and cook another 3-5 minutes or until golden browned. Serve immediately.

Nutrition Facts Per Serving
Calories 314, Total Fat 10g, Saturated Fat 4g, Total Carbs 13g, Net Carbs 12g, Protein 38g, Sugar 0g, Fiber 1g, Sodium 356mg, Potassium 355mg, Phosphorus 272mg

Pork Schnitzel

Prep time: 15 minutes, cook time: 30 minutes, Serves: 10
7 Ingredients:
- 10 pork cutlets
- 1 tsp salt
- 1 tsp pepper
- 1 cup flour
- 2 eggs
- 1 cup Panko bread crumbs
- Nonstick cooking spray

Instructions
1. Place each cutlet between plastic wrap and pound to ¼-inch thick. Sprinkle both sides with salt and pepper.
2. Place the flour in a shallow dish.
3. In a separate shallow dish, beat the eggs.
4. Place the bread crumbs in another shallow dish.
5. Place the baking pan in position 2 of the oven. Spray the fryer basket with cooking spray.
6. Dip each cutlet first in flour, then egg, then coat with bread crumbs. Place in basket in a single layer, these will need to be cooked in batches.
7. Place basket on the pan and set oven to air fry on 375°F for 10 minutes. Cook each cutlet 3-4 minutes per side, or until nicely browned. Repeat with remaining cutlets. Serve immediately.

Nutrition Facts Per Serving
Calories 320, Total Fat 8g, Saturated Fat 3g, Total Carbs 17g, Net Carbs 16g, Protein 45g, Sugar 1g, Fiber 1g, Sodium 417mg, Potassium 768mg, Phosphorus 484mg

Stuffed Bell Peppers

Prep time: 15 minutes, cook time: 15 minutes, Serves: 6

11 Ingredients:
- 6 green bell peppers, cut off tops & remove seeds
- 1 lb. lean ground beef
- 1 tbsp. olive oil
- ¼ cup green onion, chopped
- ¼ cup fresh parsley, chopped
- ½ tsp sage
- ½ tsp garlic salt
- 1 cup rice, cooked
- 1 cup marinara sauce
- Nonstick cooking spray
- ¼ cup mozzarella cheese, grated

Instructions
1. Heat a medium skillet over med-high heat. Add ground beef and cook, breaking up with spatula, until no longer pink. Drain off fat.
2. Add oil, onion, and seasonings and stir to mix.
3. Stir in rice and marinara and mix well.
4. Spoon beef mixture into the bell peppers.
5. Place the baking pan in position 2 of the oven. Lightly spray fryer basket with cooking spray.
6. Place peppers in basket and place on baking pan. Set oven to air fry on 355°F for 10 minutes.
7. Remove basket and sprinkle cheese over tops of peppers. Return to oven and cook another 5 minutes, or until peppers are tended and cheese is melted. Serve immediately.

Nutrition Facts Per Serving
Calories 398, Total Fat 16g, Saturated Fat 5g, Total Carbs 35g, Net Carbs 31g, Protein 26g, Sugar 4g, Fiber 4g, Sodium 114mg, Potassium 674mg, Phosphorus 272mg

Mixed Meat Balls

Prep time: 10 minutes, cook time: 15 minutes, Serves: 8
10 Ingredients:
- 1 lb. ground beef
- 1 lb. mild Italian sausage
- ¼ cup onion, chopped fine
- 2 cloves garlic, chopped fine
- 2 tbsp. fresh parsley, chopped
- 2 eggs
- 1½ cup parmesan cheese, grated
- ½ tsp salt
- ¼ tsp pepper
- ½ tsp crushed red pepper flakes
- ½ tsp Italian seasoning
- Nonstick cooking spray

Instructions
1. In a large bowl, combine all ingredients thoroughly.
2. Form mixture into 1-inch balls.
3. Place baking pan in position 2 of the oven. Lightly spray fryer basket with cooking spray.
4. Add meatballs in a single layer, these will need to be cooked in batches, to the basket.
5. Place basket on the baking pan and set oven to air fryer on 350°F for 15 minutes. Turn meatballs over halfway through cooking time. Serve immediately.

Nutrition Facts Per Serving
Calories 406, Total Fat 30g, Saturated Fat 12g, Total Carbs 4g, Net Carbs 4g, Protein 30g, Sugar 0g, Fiber 0g, Sodium 951mg, Potassium 379mg, Phosphorus 335mg

Dijon Roasted Lamb Chops

Prep time: 5 minutes, cook time: 15 minutes, Serves: 4

6 Ingredients:
- 8 lamb loin chops
- 2 tbsp. Dijon mustard
- 2 tbsp. extra virgin olive oil
- 2 cloves garlic, chopped fine
- 2 tsp dried Herbs de Provence
- ¼ tsp salt
- ¼ tsp pepper

Instructions
1. Line baking pan with parchment paper.
2. Lay chops, in a single layer, on prepared pan. Sprinkle with salt and pepper.
3. In a small bowl, combine remaining ingredients, mix well. Spoon mixture over tops of chops evenly.
4. Set oven to convection bake on 400°F for 20 minutes. After 5 minutes, place pan in position 1 of the oven and cook 15 minutes.
5. Remove from oven and let rest 5 minutes before serving.

Nutrition Facts Per Serving
Calories 189, Total Fat 13g, Saturated Fat 3g, Total Carbs 1g, Net Carbs 1g, Protein 17g, Sugar 0g, Fiber 0g, Sodium 296mg, Potassium 295mg, Phosphorus 170mg

Spiced Pork Roast

Prep time: 5 minutes, cook time: 50 minutes, Serves: 8

15 Ingredients:
- Nonstick cooking spray
- 3 1/3 tbsp. brown sugar
- 2/3 tbsp. sugar
- 1 ½ tsp pepper
- 1 tsp salt
- 1 tsp ginger
- ¾ tsp garlic powder
- ¾ tsp onion salt
- ½ tbsp. dry mustard
- ¼ tsp cayenne pepper
- ¼ tsp crushed red pepper flakes
- ¼ tsp cumin
- ¼ tsp paprika
- ¾ tsp thyme
- 2 ½ lb. pork loin roast, boneless

Instructions
1. Place baking pan in position 1 of the oven. Spray the fryer basket with cooking spray.
2. In a small bowl, combine sugars and spices, mix well.
3. Rub spice mixture into all sides of the pork roast. Place roast in the basket.
4. Set oven to convection bake on 300°F for 60 minutes. After 5 minutes, place the basket on the pan and cook 45-50 minutes.
5. Remove from oven and let rest 10 minutes before slicing and serving.

Nutrition Facts Per Serving
Calories 224, Total Fat 6g, Saturated Fat 2g, Total Carbs 8g, Net Carbs 8g, Protein 32g, Sugar 8g, Fiber 0g, Sodium 362mg, Potassium 549mg, Phosphorus 321mg

Chapter 5- Poultry
Buffalo Chicken Tenders

Prep time: 60 minutes, cook time: 25 minutes, Serves: 5

9 Ingredients:
- Nonstick cooking spray
- 2/3 cup panko bread crumbs
- ½ tsp cayenne pepper
- ½ tsp paprika
- ½ tsp garlic powder
- ½ tsp salt
- 3 chicken breasts, boneless, skinless & cut in 10 strips
- ½ cup butter, melted
- ½ cup hot sauce

Instructions
1. Line a baking sheet with foil and spray with cooking spray.
2. In a shallow dish combine, bread crumbs and seasonings.
3. Dip chicken in crumb mixture to coat all sides. Lay on prepared pan and refrigerate 1 hour.
4. In a small bowl, whisk together butter and hot sauce.
5. Place baking pan in position 2 of the oven. Lightly spray the fryer basket with cooking spray.
6. Dip each piece of chicken in the butter mixture and place in basket. Place the basket on the baking pan.
7. Set oven to air fry on 400°F for 25 minutes. Cook until outside is crispy and golden brown and chicken is no longer pink. Turn chicken over halfway through cooking time. Serve immediately.

Nutrition Facts Per Serving
Calories 371, Total Fat 23g, Saturated Fat 12g, Total Carbs 10g, Net Carbs 9g, Protein 31g, Sugar 1g, Fiber 1g, Sodium 733mg, Potassium 505mg, Phosphorus 310mg

Turkey Turnovers

Prep time: 10 minutes, cook time: 10 minutes, Serves: 8

6 Ingredients:
- 2 cups turkey, cooked & chopped
- 1 cup cheddar cheese, grated
- 1 cup broccoli, cooked & chopped
- ½ cup mayonnaise
- ½ tsp salt
- ¼ tsp pepper
- 2 cans refrigerated crescent rolls

Instructions
1. Place the baking pan in position 1 of the oven.
2. In a large bowl, combine all ingredients, except rolls, mix well.
3. Separate each can of rolls into 4 squares, press perforations to seal.
4. Spoon turkey mixture on center of each square. Fold over diagonally and seal the edges.
5. Set oven to bake on 375°F for 15 minutes.
6. Brush tops of turnovers lightly with additional mayonnaise. After oven has preheated 5 minutes, place turnovers on baking pan and cook 10-12 minutes or until golden brown. Serve warm.

Nutrition Facts Per Serving
Calories 309, Total Fat 21g, Saturated Fat 6g, Total Carbs 15g, Net Carbs 13g, Protein 15g, Sugar 1g, Fiber 2g, Sodium 537mg, Potassium 172mg, Phosphorus 176mg

Chicken Parm

Prep time: 10 minutes, cook time: 35 minutes, Serves: 4

12 Ingredients:
- Nonstick cooking spray
- ½ cup flour
- 2 eggs
- 2/3 cup panko bread crumbs
- 2/3 cup Italian seasoned bread crumbs
- 1/3 + ¼ cup parmesan cheese, divided
- 2 tbsp. fresh parsley, chopped
- ½ tsp salt
- ¼ tsp pepper
- 4 chicken breast halves, skinless & boneless
- 24 oz. marinara sauce
- 1 cup mozzarella cheese, grated

Instructions

1. Place the baking pan in position 2 of the oven. Lightly spray the fryer basket with cooking spray.
2. Place flour in a shallow dish.
3. In a separate shallow dish, beat the eggs.
4. In a third shallow dish, combine both bread crumbs, 1/3 cup parmesan cheese, 2 tablespoons parsley, salt, and pepper.
5. Place chicken between two sheets of plastic wrap and pound to ½-inch thick.
6. Dip chicken first in flour, then eggs, and bread crumb mixture to coat. Place in basket and place the basket on the baking pan.
7. Set oven to air fry on 375°F for 10 minutes. Turn chicken over halfway through cooking time.
8. Remove chicken and baking pan from the oven. Place the rack in position 1. Set oven to bake on 425°F for 30 minutes.
9. Pour 1 ½ cups marinara in the bottom of 8x11-inch baking dish. Place chicken over sauce and add another 2 tablespoons marinara to tops of chicken. Top chicken with mozzarella and parmesan cheese.
10. Once oven preheats for 5 minutes, place the dish in the oven and bake 20-25 minutes until bubbly and cheese is golden brown. Serve.

Nutrition Facts Per Serving

Calories 529, Total Fat 13g, Saturated Fat 5g, Total Carbs 52g, Net Carbs 47g, Protein 51g, Sugar 9g, Fiber 5g, Sodium 1437mg, Potassium 1083mg, Phosphorus 709mg

Teriyaki Duck Legs

Prep time: 15 minutes, cook time: 2 hours, Serves: 6
4 Ingredients:
- 3 lbs. duck legs
- ½ cup teriyaki sauce
- 2 tbsp. soy sauce
- 2 tbsp. malt vinegar

Instructions
1. Place the rack in position 1 of the oven.
2. Place the duck legs, skin side up, in an 8x11-inch baking dish.
3. In a small bowl, whisk together remaining ingredients and pour around duck legs. Liquid needs to reach the skin level of duck, if not add water until it does.
4. Set the oven to convection bake on 300°F for 60 minutes. After 5 minutes, place the ducks in the oven and cook 90 minutes, or until tender.
5. Remove duck from the oven. Pour off cooking liquid into a small saucepan. Skim off fat and reserve. Bring sauce to a boil and cook until it reduces down, about 10 minutes, stirring occasionally.
6. Place the baking pan in position 2 of the oven. Place the duck legs in the fryer basket and brush with reserved fat and sauce. Place the basket in the oven and set to broil on 400°F for 10 minutes. Turn duck over halfway through and brush with fat and sauce again. Serve.

Nutrition Facts Per Serving
Calories 608, Total Fat 20g, Saturated Fat 5g, Total Carbs 6g, Net Carbs 6g, Protein 101g, Sugar 5g, Fiber 0g, Sodium 1063mg, Potassium 111mg, Phosphorus 68mg

Turkey Burgers

Prep time: 10 minutes, cook time: 10 minutes, Serves: 4
7 Ingredients:
- 1 1/3 lb. ground turkey
- ½ cup gruyere cheese, grated
- 3 green onions, chopped fine
- ¼ cup bread crumbs
- ¼ cup Dijon mustard
- ½ tsp salt
- ½ tsp pepper

Instruction
1. In a large bowl, combine all ingredients until combined.
2. Form into 4 patties. Lightly spray tops with cooking spray and put them in the fryer basket, sprayed side down. Spray patties again.
3. Place the baking pan in position 2 of the oven and add basket. Set oven to air fry on 400°F for 10 minutes. Turn burgers over halfway through cooking time. Serve.

Nutrition Facts Per Serving
Calories 321, Total Fat 17g, Saturated Fat 6g, Total Carbs 7g, Net Carbs 6g, Protein 35g, Sugar 1g, Fiber 1g, Sodium 697mg, Potassium 436mg, Phosphorus 415mg

Spicy Chicken Nuggets

Prep time: 15 minutes, cook time: 10 minutes, Serves: 6

13 Ingredients:
- Nonstick cooking spray
- ¼ cup mayonnaise
- 2 tbsp. sweet chili sauce
- 1 tbsp. honey
- 1 tbsp. + 2 tsp hot sauce, divided
- 1 cup buttermilk
- ¾ cup flour
- ½ cup cornstarch
- 1 egg
- ½ tsp salt
- ¼ tsp pepper
- 1 cup panko bread crumbs
- 1 lb. chicken breasts, boneless, skinless & cut in 1-inch pieces

Instructions

1. Place the baking pan in position 2 of the oven. Lightly spray the fryer basket with cooking spray.
2. In a small bowl, whisk together mayonnaise, chili sauce, honey and 2 teaspoons hot sauce. Cover until ready to use.
3. In a large bowl, whisk together buttermilk, flour, cornstarch, egg, remaining hot sauce, salt, and pepper.
4. Place bread crumbs in a shallow dish.
5. One at a time, dip the chicken into buttermilk mixture then roll in bread crumbs to coat. Place in fryer basket in a single layer, these will need to be cooked in batches. Lightly spray the nuggets with cooking spray.
6. Place basket in the oven and set to air fry on 375°F for 10 minutes. Cook chicken until gold brown outside and no longer pink inside, turning over halfway through cooking time. Repeat with remaining chicken pieces.
7. Serve drizzled with reserved sauce.

Nutrition Facts Per Serving

Calories 459, Total Fat 11g, Saturated Fat 2g, Total Carbs 41g, Net Carbs 39g, Protein 24g, Sugar 7g, Fiber 2g, Sodium 615mg, Potassium 409mg, Phosphorus 268mg

Turkey Meatloaf

Prep time: 5 minutes, cook time: 55 minutes, Serves: 4

9 Ingredients:
- ¼ cup + 2 tbsp. ketchup, divided
- 2 tsp Worcestershire sauce
- 1 tsp olive oil
- ½ onion, chopped fine
- 1 1/3 lbs. lean ground turkey
- ½ cup bread crumbs, seasoned
- 1 egg
- 1 tsp salt
- 1 tsp marjoram

Instructions
1. Place rack in position 1 of the oven.
2. In a small bowl, stir together 2 tablespoons ketchup and Worcestershire sauce.
3. Heat oil in a small skillet over low heat. Add onion and cook until translucent, about 3-5 minutes. Remove from heat.
4. In a medium bowl, combine turkey, onion, bread crumbs, egg, salt, marjoram, and remaining ketchup. Transfer mixture to an 8-inch loaf pan. Spread sauce over top.
5. Set oven to bake on 350°F for 60 minutes. After 5 minutes, place turkey loaf in the oven and bake 55-60 minutes.
6. Remove from oven and let rest 5 minutes before slicing and serving.

Nutrition Facts Per Serving
Calories 354, Total Fat 16g, Saturated Fat 4g, Total Carbs 18g, Net Carbs 17g, Protein 32g, Sugar 6g, Fiber 1g, Sodium 1112mg, Potassium 472mg, Phosphorus 353mg

Lacquered Duck Breasts

Prep time: 5 minutes, cook time: 15 minutes, Serves: 4
6 Ingredients:
- 2 Margret duck breasts
- ¾ tsp salt, divided
- ¼ tsp pepper
- 4 tbsp. honey
- 3 tbsp. balsamic vinegar
- ¼ tsp cinnamon

Instructions
1. Place the baking pan in position 1 of the oven.
2. With a sharp knife, score the skin of the duck, don't cut through to the flesh. Sprinkle both sides with ½ teaspoon salt and pepper.
3. Heat a large skillet over med-high heat. Add the duck, skin side down, and cook 5-6 minutes, or until fat is rendered. Transfer duck to a plate and keep warm.
4. Drain the fat from the skillet. Add honey and vinegar and deglaze the pan, stirring up the browned bits from the bottom. Simmer mixture 2-3 minutes until it starts to thicken. Stir in ¼ teaspoon salt and cinnamon.
5. Set the oven to convection bake on 375°F for 15 minutes.
6. Add the duck to the skillet and turn to coat with sauce. After the oven has preheated for 5 minutes, place the duck on the baking pan and pour a little sauce over the top. Cook another 7-10 minutes, turning duck over and adding more sauce halfway through, until duck reaches medium rare. Slice and serve immediately.

Nutrition Facts Per Serving
Calories 184, Total Fat 4g, Saturated Fat 1g, Total Carbs 20g, Net Carbs 20g, Protein 17g, Sugar 19g, Fiber 0g, Sodium 487mg, Potassium 250mg, Phosphorus 158mg

Copycat Chicken Sandwich

Prep time: 15 minutes, cook time: 15 minutes, Serves: 4

14 Ingredients:
- 2 chicken breasts, boneless & skinless
- 1 cup buttermilk
- 1 tbsp. + 2 tsp paprika, divided
- 1 tbsp. + 1 ½ tsp garlic powder, divided
- 2 tsp salt, divided
- 2 tsp pepper, divided
- 4 brioche buns
- 1 cup flour
- ½ cup corn starch
- 1 tbsp. onion powder
- 1 tbsp. cayenne pepper
- ½ cup mayonnaise
- 1 tsp hot sauce
- Sliced pickles

Instructions

1. Place chicken between two sheets of plastic wrap and pound to ½-inch thick. Cut crosswise to get 4 cutlets.
2. In a large bowl, whisk together buttermilk and one teaspoon each paprika, garlic powder, salt, and pepper. Add chicken, cover, and refrigerate overnight.
3. Place the buns on the baking pan and place in position 2 of the oven. Set to toast for about 2-5 minutes depending how toasted you want them. Set aside.
4. In a medium shallow dish, combine flour, cornstarch, onion powder, cayenne pepper, and remaining paprika, garlic powder, salt, and pepper.
5. Whisk in 2-3 tablespoons of the buttermilk batter chicken was marinating in until smooth.
6. Lightly spray fryer basket with cooking spray.
7. Dredge chicken in the flour mixture forming a thick coating of the batter. Place in fryer basket.
8. Place basket in the oven. Set oven to air fryer on 375°F for 10 minutes. Cook until crispy and golden brown, turning chicken over halfway through cooking time.
9. In a small bowl, whisk together mayonnaise, hot sauce, 1 teaspoon paprika, and ½ teaspoon garlic powder.
10. To serve, spread top of buns with mayonnaise mixture. Place chicken on bottom buns and top with pickles then top bun.

Nutrition Facts Per Serving

Calories 689, Total Fat 27g, Saturated Fat 5g, Total Carbs 71g, Net Carbs 67g, Protein 38g, Sugar 7g, Fiber 4g, Sodium 1734mg, Potassium 779mg, Phosphorus 435mg

Mini Pot Pies

Prep time: 15 minutes, cook time: 20 minutes, Serves: 16

5 Ingredients:
- 2 cans large flaky biscuits, refrigerated
- 6 oz. turkey, cooked & chopped fine
- 3 ½ cups turkey gravy
- 2 cups mixed vegetables
- 1 cup cheddar cheese, grated

Instructions

1. Place baking pan in position 1 of the oven. Spray 3 6-cup muffin tins with cooking spray.
2. Gently pull each biscuit until it is double in size. Press into prepared tins, pressing up the sides until edge is at, or above, the top of the cup.
3. In a large bowl, stir together turkey, gravy, and vegetables. Spoon mixture into biscuits. Top with cheese.
4. Set oven to bake on 350°F for 25 minutes. After 5 minutes, place muffin tin, one at a time, in the oven and bake until golden brown, about 20-22 minutes. Repeat with remaining tins. Serve warm.

Nutrition Facts Per Serving

Calories 324, Total Fat 8g, Saturated Fat 2g, Total Carbs 24g, Net Carbs 23g, Protein 9g, Sugar 1g, Fiber 1g, Sodium 790mg, Potassium 210mg, Phosphorus 232mg

Popcorn Turkey

Prep time: 10 minutes, cook time: 10 minutes, Serves: 4

7 Ingredients:
- Nonstick cooking spray
- 1 cup flour
- 2 eggs
- ½ cup milk
- 2 tbsp. Cajun seasoning
- 2 cups bread crumbs
- 1 large turkey breast, cut in 1-inch pieces

Instructions

1. Place the baking pan in position 2 of the oven. Lightly spray the fryer basket with cooking spray.
2. In a large bowl, whisk together flour, eggs, milk, and seasoning.
3. Place bread crumbs in a shallow dish.
4. Add the turkey to the batter and stir to coat. Roll each piece of turkey in the bread crumbs and place them in the fryer basket, these may need to be cooked in batches. Spray them lightly with cooking spray.
5. Place the basket in the oven and set to air fry on 375°F for 10 minutes. Cook turkey nuggets until crisp and golden brown, turning over halfway through cooking time. Serve with your favorite dipping sauce.

Nutrition Facts Per Serving
Calories 655, Total Fat 11g, Saturated Fat 3g, Total Carbs 64g, Net Carbs 61g, Protein 78g, Sugar 5g, Fiber 3g, Sodium 690mg, Potassium 855mg, Phosphorus 744mg

Italian Chicken Casserole

Prep time: 15 minutes, cook time: 30 minutes, Serves: 4

14 Ingredients:
- Nonstick cooking spray.
- 2 tbsp. olive oil
- 1 cup chicken breasts, boneless, skinless & cut in 1-inch pieces
- 2/3 onion, chopped
- 1 clove garlic, chopped fine
- 1 cup elbow macaroni, cook according to pkg. directions, drain
- 14 ½ oz. tomatoes, diced
- 1 ¼ cups mozzarella cheese, grated
- ¼ cup fresh parsley, chopped
- ½ tsp salt
- ¼ tsp pepper
- ¼ cup bread crumbs
- 1/3 cup parmesan cheese, grated
- 2 tbsp. butter, melted

Instructions

1. Place the rack in position 1 of the oven. Spray an 8-inch square baking dish with cooking spray.
2. Heat oil in a medium skillet over medium heat. Add chicken and cook 3 minutes, stirring occasionally.
3. And onions and garlic and cook until onions are soft and chicken is no longer pink, about 5 minutes.
4. In a large bowl, combine pasta and chicken. Stir in tomatoes with their juice, mozzarella cheese, parsley, salt, and pepper. Transfer to prepared baking dish.
5. Set oven to bake on 400°F for 35 minutes.
6. In a small bowl, stir together bread crumbs, parmesan cheese, and butter. Sprinkle on top of casserole.
7. Once oven has preheated for 5 minutes, add casserole and bake 30 minutes until top is golden brown. Serve.

Nutrition Facts Per Serving

Calories 427, Total Fat 17g, Saturated Fat 6g, Total Carbs 36g, Net Carbs 32g, Protein 30g, Sugar 7g, Fiber 4g, Sodium 1011mg, Potassium 560mg, Phosphorus 463mg

Roast Duck

Prep time: 10 minutes, cook time: 1 hour, Serves: 6

6 Ingredients:
- 3 lb. duck
- 1 tsp salt
- 3 tbsp. crushed red pepper flakes
- 3 tbsp. soy sauce, divided
- 3 tbsp. honey
- 2 tbsp. rice vinegar

Instructions

1. Wash the duck and pat dry with paper towels. Place in an 8x11-inch baking dish.
2. In a small bowl, stir together salt and pepper flakes. Rub over the skin of the duck. Sprinkle 2 tablespoons soy sauce over duck. Cover and refrigerate 2 hours.
3. Place rack in position 1 and set oven to convection bake on 375°F for 5 minutes.
4. In a small bowl, whisk together honey, vinegar, and remaining soy sauce. Brush over duck.
5. Once the oven has preheated, place duck inside and cook 1 hour. Serve.

Nutrition Facts Per Serving

Calories 519, Total Fat 35g, Saturated Fat 11g, Total Carbs 11g, Net Carbs 10g, Protein 40g, Sugar 9g, Fiber 1g, Sodium 772mg, Potassium 652mg, Phosphorus 401mg

Sweet & Spicy Chicken

Prep time: 10 minutes, cook time: 30 minutes, Serves: 6

12 Ingredients:
- 6 chicken breasts, skinless, boneless, cut in 1-inch pieces
- 1 cup corn starch
- 2 cups water
- 1 cup ketchup
- ½ cup brown sugar
- 1 tbsp. sesame oil
- 3 tbsp. soy sauce
- 2 tbsp. black sesame seeds
- 2 tbsp. white sesame seeds
- ½ tsp red pepper flakes
- ½ tsp garlic powder
- 2 tbsp. green onion, chopped

Instructions
1. Place baking pan in position 2. Lightly spray fryer basket with cooking spray.
2. Place the cornstarch in a large bowl. Add chicken and toss to coat chicken thoroughly.
3. Working in batches, place chicken in a single layer in the basket and place on baking pan. Set oven to air fryer on 350°F for 10 minutes. Stir the chicken halfway through cooking time. Transfer chicken to baking sheet.
4. In a large skillet over medium heat, whisk together remaining ingredients, except green onion. Bring to a boil, stirring occasionally. Cook until sauce has thickened, about 3-5 minutes.
5. Add chicken and stir to coat. Cook another 3-5 minutes, stirring frequently. Serve garnished with green onions.

Nutrition Facts Per Serving
Calories 556, Total Fat 12g, Saturated Fat 3g, Total Carbs 50g, Net Carbs 49g, Protein 62g, Sugar 26g, Fiber 1g, Sodium 730mg, Potassium 957mg, Phosphorus 569mg

Guacamole Stuffed Chicken

Prep time: 10 minutes, cook time: 10 minutes, Serves: 4
6 Ingredients:
- Nonstick cooking spray
- 2 chicken breasts, boneless & skinless
- ½ cup guacamole
- 2/3 cup cheddar cheese, grated
- 1 cup panko bread crumbs
- ½ tsp Adobo seasoning

Instructions
1. Place baking pan in position 2. Spray the fryer basket with cooking spray.
2. Cut the chicken breasts in half, similar to butterflying them but cut all the way through. Place the chicken between two sheets of plastic wrap and pound really thin.
3. Spread 2 tablespoons guacamole over each piece of chicken. Sprinkle with the cheese. Fold the chicken pieces in half covering the filling.
4. In a shallow dish, combine bread crumbs and seasoning. Coat each side of chicken with mixture and place in the fryer basket.
5. Place the basket in the oven and set to air fry on 375°F for 10 minutes. Turn chicken over halfway through cooking time. Serve immediately.

Nutrition Facts Per Serving
Calories 363, Total Fat 15g, Saturated Fat 5g, Total Carbs 22g, Net Carbs 19g, Protein 35g, Sugar 2g, Fiber 3g, Sodium 441mg, Potassium 604mg, Phosphorus 400mg

Chapter 6 – Vegetarian & Vegan

Crispy Potato Lentil Nuggets

Prep time: 25 minutes, cook time: 10 minutes, Serves: 4

11 Ingredients:
- Nonstick cooking spray
- 1 cup red lentils
- 1 tbsp. olive oil
- 1 cup onion, grated
- 1 cup carrot, grated
- 1 cup potato, grated
- ½ cup flour
- ½ tsp salt
- ½ tsp garlic powder
- ¾ tsp paprika
- ¼ tsp pepper

Instructions
1. Place baking pan in position 2. Lightly spray fryer basket with cooking spray.
2. Soak lentils in just enough water to cover them for 25 minutes.
3. Heat oil in a large skillet over medium heat. Add onion, carrot, and potato. Cook, stirring frequently until vegetables are tender, 12-15 minutes.
4. Drain the lentils and place them in a food processor. Add flour and spices and pulse to combine, leave some texture to the mixture.
5. Add cooked veggies to the food processor and pulse just until combined. Mixture will be sticky, so oil your hands. Form mixture into nugget shapes and add to the fryer basket in a single layer.
6. Place basket in the oven and set air fry on 350°F for 10 minutes. Turn nuggets over halfway through cooking time. Repeat with remaining mixture. Serve with your favorite dipping sauce.

Nutrition Facts Per Serving
Calories 317, Total Fat 5g, Saturated Fat 1g, Total Carbs 54g, Net Carbs 46g, Protein 14g, Sugar 3g, Fiber 8g, Sodium 317mg, Potassium 625mg, Phosphorus 197mg

Portobello Steaks

Prep time: 5 minutes, cook time: 20 minutes, Serves: 4

5 Ingredients:
- Nonstick cooking spray
- ¼ cup olive oil
- 2 tbsp. steak seasoning, unsalted
- 1 rosemary stem
- 4 Portobello mushrooms, large caps with stems removed

Instructions
1. Place baking pan in position 2 and spray with cooking spray.
2. In a large bowl, stir together oil, steak seasoning, and rosemary.
3. Add mushrooms and toss to coat all sides thoroughly.
4. Set oven to bake on 400°F for 25 minutes. After 5 minutes, place the mushrooms on the pan and bake 20 minutes, or until mushrooms are tender. Serve immediately.

Nutrition Facts Per Serving
Calories 142, Total Fat 14g, Saturated Fat 2g, Total Carbs 3g, Net Carbs 2g, Protein 1g, Sugar 1g, Fiber 1g, Sodium 309mg, Potassium 118mg, Phosphorus 20mg

Vegan Meatloaf

Prep time: 10 minutes, cook time: 65 minutes, Serves: 8

18 Ingredients:
- Nonstick cooking spray
- 3 1/3 cups chickpeas, cooked
- 1 onion, chopped fine
- 2 stalks celery, chopped
- 2 carrots, chopped fine
- 2 cloves garlic diced fine
- 2 cups panko bread crumbs
- ½ cup almond milk, unsweetened
- 3 tbsp. vegan Worcestershire sauce
- 3 tbsp. soy sauce, divided
- 2 tbsp. olive oil
- 2 tbsp. flax seeds, ground
- ¼ cup + 2 tbsp. tomato paste
- 1 tsp liquid smoke
- ¼ tsp pepper
- 2 tbsp. maple syrup
- 2 tbsp. apple cider vinegar
- 1 tsp paprika

Instructions
1. Place rack in position 1. Lightly spray a 9-inch loaf pan with cooking spray.
2. Place chickpeas, onion, celery, carrots, cloves, bread crumbs, milk, Worcestershire, 2 tablespoons soy sauce, oil, flax seeds, 2 tablespoons tomato paste, liquid smoke, and pepper in a food processor, you may need to do this in batches. Pulse until ingredients are combined but don't over blend. Transfer each batch to a large bowl, then mix together.
3. Set oven to bake on 375°F for 35 minutes.
4. Press mixture into the prepared pan. After the oven has preheated 5 minutes, add loaf pan to the oven and bake 30 minutes.
5. In a small bowl, whisk together remaining tomato paste and soy sauce, along with the syrup, vinegar, and paprika until smooth.
6. When the timer goes off, remove the loaf from the oven. Spoon glaze over top and bake another 20-25 minutes. Let cool 10 minutes before slicing and serving.

Nutrition Facts Per Serving
Calories 623, Total Fat 11g, Saturated Fat 2g, Total Carbs 83g, Net Carbs 70g, Protein 23g, Sugar 18g, Fiber 13g, Sodium 501mg, Potassium 969mg, Phosphorus 317mg

Teriyaki Tofu

Prep time: 10 minutes, cook time: 15 minutes, Serves 3

8 Ingredients:
- Nonstick cooking spray
- 14 oz. firm or extra firm tofu, pressed & cut in 1-inch cubes
- ¼ cup cornstarch
- ½ tsp salt
- ½ tsp ginger
- ½ tsp white pepper
- 3 tbsp. olive oil
- 12 oz. bottle vegan teriyaki sauce

Instructions
1. Lightly spray baking pan with cooking spray.
2. In a shallow dish, combine cornstarch, salt, ginger, and pepper.
3. Heat oil in a large skillet over med-high heat.
4. Toss tofu cubes in cornstarch mixture then add to skillet. Cook 5 minutes, turning over halfway through, until tofu is nicely seared. Transfer the tofu to the prepared baking pan.
5. Set oven to convection bake on 350°F for 15 minutes.
6. Pour all but ½ cup teriyaki sauce over tofu and stir to coat. After oven has preheated for 5 minutes, place the baking pan in position 2 and bake tofu 10 minutes.
7. Turn tofu over, spoon the sauce in the pan over it and bake another 10 minutes. Serve with reserved sauce for dipping.

Nutrition Facts Per Serving
Calories 469, Total Fat 25g, Saturated Fat 4g, Total Carbs 33g, Net Carbs 30g, Protein 28g, Sugar 16g, Fiber 3g, Sodium 2424mg, Potassium 571mg, Phosphorus 428mg

Butter Burgers

Prep time: 25 minutes, cook time: 30 minutes, Serves: 4

12 Ingredients:
- Nonstick cooking spray
- ½ cup black beans, rinsed & drained
- 12 oz. mushrooms, sliced
- 1 ½ cup brown rice, cooked
- ½ cup oats
- 1 tsp salt
- ½ tsp pepper
- 1 tsp garlic powder
- 1 tsp onion powder
- ¼ tsp red pepper flakes
- ¼ cup Vegan butter
- 2 cups onions, sliced

Instructions

1. Place baking pan in position 2 in the oven. Lightly spray fryer basket with cooking spray.
2. Pat the beans with paper towel to get them as dry as possible.
3. Heat a medium skillet over med-high heat. Add mushrooms and cook, stirring frequently, until almost no moisture remains.
4. Add mushrooms, beans, rice, oats, and seasonings to a food processor. Pulse to chop and combine ingredients. Do not over blend. Let mixture rest 20 minutes.
5. Melt butter in a large skillet over medium heat. Add onions and cook until browned and tender.
6. Form mushroom mixture into 4 patties and place in the fryer basket. Place in oven and set to air fry on 350°F for 10 minutes. Cook burgers 8-10 minutes, until nicely browned, turning over halfway through cooking time.
7. Serve on toasted buns topped with cooked onions.

Nutrition Facts Per Serving

Calories 351, Total Fat 15g, Saturated Fat 8g, Total Carbs 44g, Net Carbs 37g, Protein 10g, Sugar 4g, Fiber 7g, Sodium 704mg, Potassium 604mg, Phosphorus 286mg

Spaghetti Squash Lasagna

Prep time: 20 minutes, cook time: 15 minutes, Serves: 4

11 Ingredients:
- 3 lb. spaghetti squash, halved lengthwise & seeded
- 4 tbsp. water, divided
- 1 tbsp. extra-virgin olive oil
- 1 bunch broccolini, chopped
- 4 cloves garlic, chopped fine
- ¼ tsp crushed red pepper flakes
- 1 cup mozzarella cheese, grated & divided
- ¼ cup parmesan cheese, grated & divided
- ¾ tsp Italian seasoning
- ½ tsp salt
- ¼ tsp ground pepper

Instructions

1. Place squash, cut side down, in a microwave safe dish. Add 2 tablespoons water and microwave on high until tender, about 10 minutes.
2. Heat oil in a large skillet over medium heat. Add broccoli, garlic, and red pepper. Cook, stirring frequently, 2 minutes.
3. Add remaining water and cook until broccolini is tender, about 3-5 minutes. Transfer to a large bowl.
4. With a fork, scrape the squash from the shells into the bowl with the broccolini. Place the shells in an 8x11-inch baking pan.
5. Add ¾ cup mozzarella, 2 tablespoons parmesan, and seasonings to the squash mixture and stir to combine. Spoon evenly into the shells and top with remaining cheese.
6. Place rack in position 1 and set oven to bake on 450°F for 15 minutes. After 5 minutes, place the squash in the oven and cook 10 minutes.
7. Set the oven to broil on high and move the pan to position 2. Broil until cheese starts to brown, about 2 minutes. Serve immediately.

Nutrition Facts Per Serving

Calories 328, Total Fat 6g, Saturated Fat 2g, Total Carbs 48g, Net Carbs 39g, Protein 18g, Sugar 3g, Fiber 9g, Sodium 674mg, Potassium 1714mg, Phosphorus 452mg

Green Chili Taquitos

Prep time: 5 minutes, cook time: 10 minutes, Serves: 3

5 Ingredients:
- Nonstick cooking spray
- 6 corn tortillas
- ¾ cup vegan cream cheese
- 1 cup vegan cheddar cheese, grated
- 4 oz. green chilies, diced & drained

Instructions

1. Place baking pan in position 2. Lightly spray fryer basket with cooking spray.
2. Wrap tortillas in paper towels and microwave 1 minute.
3. Spread the cream cheese over tortillas. Top with cheddar cheese and chilies. Roll up tightly. Place, seam side down, in fryer basket.
4. Place the basket on the baking pan and set oven to air fry on 350°F for 10 minutes or until tortillas are browned and crispy. Turn taquitos over halfway through cooking time. Serve immediately.

Nutrition Facts Per Serving

Calories 706, Total Fat 34g, Saturated Fat 18g, Total Carbs 51g, Net Carbs 35g, Protein 24g, Sugar 11g, Fiber 16g, Sodium 2371mg, Potassium 1074mg, Phosphorus 850mg

Chickpea Fritters

Prep time: 5 minutes, cook time: 10 minutes, Serves: 4

7 Ingredients:
- Nonstick cooking spray
- 1 cup chickpeas, cooked
- 1 onion, chopped
- ¼ tsp salt
- ¼ tsp pepper
- ¼ tsp turmeric
- ¼ tsp coriander

Instructions
1. Place the baking pan in position 2. Lightly spray the fryer basket with cooking spray.
2. Add the onion to a food processor and pulse until finely diced.
3. Add remaining ingredients and pulse until combined but not pureed.
4. Form the mixture into 8 patties and place them in the fryer basket, these may need to be cooked in two batches.
5. Place the basket in the oven and set to air fry on 350°F for 10 minutes. Cook fritters until golden brown and crispy, turning over halfway through cooking time. Serve with your favorite dipping sauce.

Nutrition Facts Per Serving

Calories 101, Total Fat 1g, Saturated Fat 0g, Total Carbs 14g, Net Carbs 10g, Protein 4g, Sugar 3g, Fiber 4g, Sodium 149mg, Potassium 159mg, Phosphorus 77mg

Roasted Fall Veggies

Prep time: 10 minutes, cook time: 30 minutes, Serves: 6
14 Ingredients:
- 2 cups sweet potatoes, cubed
- 2 cups Brussel sprouts, halved
- 3 cups button mushrooms, halved
- ½ red onion, chopped
- 3 cloves garlic, chopped fine
- 4 sage leaves, chopped
- 2 sprigs rosemary, chopped
- 2 sprigs thyme, chopped
- 1 tsp garlic powder
- 1 tsp onion powder
- ½ tsp salt
- ¼ tsp pepper
- 3 tbsp. balsamic vinegar
- Nonstick cooking spray

Instructions
1. Chop vegetables so that they are as close to equal in size as possible. Roughly chop the herbs.
2. In a large bowl, toss vegetables, herbs, and spices to mix. Drizzle vinegar overall and toss to coat.
3. Spray the baking pan with cooking spray. Set oven to bake on 350°F for 35 minutes.
4. Transfer the vegetable mixture to the baking pan and after 5 minutes, place in the oven in position 1. Bake vegetables 25-30 minutes or until vegetables are tender. Turn them over halfway through cooking. Serve immediately.

Nutrition Facts Per Serving
Calories 76, Total Fat 0g, Saturated Fat 0g, Total Carbs 16g, Net Carbs 13g, Protein 3g, Sugar 5g, Fiber 3g, Sodium 231mg, Potassium 455mg, Phosphorus 92mg

Asian Tofu "Meatballs"

Prep time: 20 minutes, cook time: 10 minutes, Serves: 4

15 Ingredients:
- 3 dried shitake mushrooms
- Nonstick cooking spray
- 14 oz. firm tofu, drained & pressed
- ¼ cup carrots, cooked
- ¼ cup bamboo shoots, sliced thin
- ½ cup Panko bread crumbs
- 2 tbsp. corn starch
- 3 ½ tablespoon soy sauce, divided
- 1 tsp garlic powder
- ¼ tsp salt
- 1/8 tsp pepper
- 1 tbsp. olive oil
- 2 tbsp. garlic, diced fine
- 2 tbsp. ketchup
- 2 tsp sugar

Instructions

1. Place the shitake mushrooms in a bowl and add just enough water to cover. Let soak 20 minutes until soft. Drain well and chop.
2. Place the baking pan in position 2. Lightly spray the fryer basket with cooking spray.
3. Place mushrooms, tofu, carrots, bamboo shoots, bread crumbs, corn starch, 1 ½ tablespoons soy sauce, and seasonings in a food processor. Pulse until thoroughly combined. Form mixture into 1-inch balls.
4. Place balls in fryer basket, these may need to be cooked in batches, and place in oven. Set to air fry on 380°F for 10 minutes. Turn the balls around halfway through cooking time.
5. Heat oil in a saucepan over medium heat. Add garlic and cook 1 minute.
6. Stir in remaining soy sauce, ketchup, and sugar. Bring to a simmer and cook until sauce thickens, 3-5 minutes.
7. When the meatballs are done, add them to sauce and stir to coat. Serve immediately.

Nutrition Facts Per Serving

Calories 305, Total Fat 13g, Saturated Fat 2g, Total Carbs 28g, Net Carbs 24g, Protein 20g, Sugar 5g, Fiber 4g, Sodium 789mg, Potassium 470mg, Phosphorus 260mg

Chapter 7 - Desserts

Cinnamon Cheesecake Bars

Prep time: 15 minutes, cook time: 30 minutes, Serves: 12
7 Ingredients:
- Nonstick cooking spray
- 16 oz. cream cheese, soft
- 1 tsp vanilla
- 1 ¼ cups sugar, divided
- 2 tubes refrigerated crescent rolls
- 1 tsp cinnamon
- ¼ cup butter

Instructions
1. Place the rack in position 1. Spray the bottom of an 8x11-inch pan with cooking spray.
2. In a medium bowl, beat cream cheese, vanilla, and ¾ cup sugar until smooth.
3. Roll out one can of crescent rolls on the bottom of prepared pan, sealing the perforations and pressing partway up the sides.
4. Spread cream cheese mixture evenly over crescents.
5. Roll out second can of crescents over the top of cheese mixture, sealing the perforations.
6. In a small bowl, stir together cinnamon and remaining sugar. Melt the butter.
7. Set oven to bake on 375°F for 35 minutes.
8. Sprinkle the cinnamon sugar over the top of the crescents and drizzle with melted butter.
9. After the oven has preheated for 5 minutes, place the pan in the oven and bake 30 minutes until the top is golden brown.
10. Cool completely. Cover and refrigerate at least 2 hours before slicing and serving.

Nutrition Facts Per Serving
Calories 332, Total Fat 18g, Saturated Fat 10g, Total Carbs 35g, Net Carbs 35g, Protein 5g, Sugar 23g, Fiber 0g, Sodium 278mg, Potassium 87mg, Phosphorus 70mg

Strawberry Cobbler

Prep time: 10 minutes, cook time: 25 minutes, Serves: 4
10 Ingredients:
- Butter flavored cooking spray
- 2 tbsp. cornstarch
- ¼ cup fresh lemon juice
- ½ cup + 1 tbsp. sugar divided
- 3 cups strawberries, hulled & sliced
- 5 tbsp. butter, cold & diced
- 1 cup flour
- 1 ½ tsp baking powder
- ½ tsp salt
- ½ cup heavy cream

Instructions
1. Place rack in position 1. Spray a 9-inch baking pan with cooking spray.
2. In a saucepan, combine cornstarch, lemon juice, and ½ cup sugar. Cook over medium heat, stirring frequently, until sugar dissolves and mixture thickens.
3. Remove from heat and gently stir in berries. Pour into prepared pan and dot with 2 tablespoons butter.
4. In a large bowl, combine flour, remaining sugar, baking powder, and salt. Using a fork or pastry cutter, cut in remaining butter until mixture resembles coarse crumbs.
5. Stir in the cream and sprinkle over strawberries.
6. Set oven to bake on 400°F for 30 minutes. After 5 minutes, place cobbler in oven and bake 25 minutes until bubbly and golden brown. Let cool at least 10 minutes before serving.

Nutrition Facts Per Serving
Calories 457, Total Fat 21g, Saturated Fat 13g, Total Carbs 63g, Net Carbs 60g, Protein 4g, Sugar 31g, Fiber 3g, Sodium 415mg, Potassium 420mg, Phosphorus 204mg

Banana Brownies

Prep time: 15 minutes, cook time: 20 minutes, Serves: 12

8 Ingredients:
- ¼ cup butter, unsalted
- 4 oz. white chocolate, chopped
- 2 bananas, mashed
- ½ cup sugar
- 1 egg
- ¼ tsp salt
- 1 tsp vanilla
- 1 cup flour

Instructions
1. Place rack in position 1.
2. In a microwave safe bowl, add butter and chocolate and microwave in 30 second intervals until melted, stirring after each cook time.
3. Stir in bananas, eggs, salt, and vanilla until combined. Stir in flour and mix well.
4. Set oven to bake on 350°F for 25 minutes.
5. Spread batter in prepared pan. After oven preheats for 5 minutes, place brownies in oven and bake 15-20 minutes or brownies pass the toothpick test.
6. Let cool 15 minutes before slicing.

Nutrition Facts Per Serving
Calories 180, Total Fat 6g, Saturated Fat 4g, Total Carbs 26g, Net Carbs 25g, Protein 3g, Sugar 16g, Fiber 1g, Sodium 65mg, Potassium 118mg, Phosphorus 42mg

Caramel Apple Cake

Prep time: 20 minutes, cook time: 55 minutes, Serves: 12

11 Ingredients:
- 1 cup coconut oil, melted
- 2 cups sugar
- 3 eggs
- 1 ½ tsp vanilla
- 2 cups flour
- 1 tsp salt
- 1 tsp baking soda
- 3 cups apples, peeled & chopped
- ½ cup butter
- 1 cup brown sugar
- ¼ cup milk

Instructions
1. Place rack in position 1. Spray an 8x11-inch pan with cooking spray.
2. In a large bowl, beat oil, sugar, eggs, and vanilla until smooth.
3. Add flour, salt, and baking soda and stir to combine. Fold in apples.
4. Set oven to bake on 350°F for 60 minutes.
5. Pour batter in prepared pan. After oven has preheated for 5 minutes, put cake in oven and bake 55-60 minutes, or until it passes the toothpick test. Let cool completely.
6. In a saucepan, over medium heat, combine butter, brown sugar, and milk. Stirring constantly, bring to a boil. Let boil, without stirring, 3 minutes. Remove from heat and spread over top of cake. Let sit 1 hour before serving.

Nutrition Facts Per Serving
Calories 553, Total Fat 27g, Saturated Fat 21g, Total Carbs 71g, Net Carbs 70g, Protein 4g, Sugar 54g, Fiber 1g, Sodium 385mg, Potassium 99mg, Phosphorus 58mg

Rocky Road Squares

Prep time: 15 minutes, cook time: 15 minutes, Serves: 16

8 Ingredients:
- 3 oz. dark chocolate, chopped
- 1/2 cup butter
- 2 cups graham cracker crumbs
- 1 cup walnuts, chopped, divided
- 1 cup coconut, divided
- ½ cup mini semi-sweet chocolate chips
- 1 ½ cups mini marshmallows
- ½ can sweetened condensed milk

Instructions
1. Place rack in position 1. Line an 8-inch square pan with parchment paper.
2. In a microwave safe bowl, place the chocolate and butter and microwave on high in 30 second intervals until melted and smooth, stirring after each interval.
3. Stir in crumbs, ½ cup nuts, and ½ cup coconut and mix well. Press evenly on the bottom of prepared pan.
4. Sprinkle the following over crust, in this order, marshmallows, coconut, remaining nuts, and chocolate chips. Drizzle milk evenly over the top.
5. Set oven to bake on 350°F for 25 minutes. After 5 minutes, add the pan to the oven and bake 15-20 minutes or until marshmallows are golden brown.
6. Remove from oven and let cool completely. Cover and refrigerate at least 1 hour before cutting and serving.

Nutrition Facts Per Serving
Calories 323, Total Fat 17g, Saturated Fat 7g, Total Carbs 36g, Net Carbs 34g, Protein 4g, Sugar 21g, Fiber 2g, Sodium 139mg, Potassium 203mg, Phosphorus 106mg

Cappuccino Blondies

Prep time: 10 minutes, cook time: 30 minutes, Serves: 16

8 Ingredients:
- Nonstick cooking spray
- 1 cup butter, soft
- 2 cups brown sugar
- 2 eggs
- 2 tsp baking powder
- 1 tsp salt
- 4 tsp espresso powder
- 2 2/3 cups flour

Instructions

1. Place rack in position 1. Lightly spray an 8x11-inch baking pan with cooking spray.
2. In a large bowl, beat together butter and sugar. Add eggs and beat until light and fluffy.
3. Add baking powder, salt, and espresso and mix well. Stir in flour until combined.
4. Set oven to bake on 350°F for 35 minutes.
5. Spread batter in prepared pan. Once oven has preheated, place brownies in oven and bake 25-30 minutes.
6. Remove from oven and let cool before cutting.

Nutrition Facts Per Serving

Calories 296, Total Fat 12g, Saturated Fat 7g, Total Carbs 44g, Net Carbs 43g, Protein 3g, Sugar 28g, Fiber 1g, Sodium 254mg, Potassium 137mg, Phosphorus 82mg

Mini Pecan Pies

Prep time: 15 minutes, cook time: 10 minutes, Serves: 8
6 Ingredients:
- Nonstick cooking spray
- 1 sheet puff pastry, thawed
- 4 tbsp. brown sugar
- ½ stick butter, melted
- 2 tbsp. maple syrup
- ½ cup pecans, chopped fine

Instructions
1. Place baking pan in position 2. Lightly spray fryer basket with cooking spray.
2. In a plastic bowl, stir together butter, syrup and pecans. Freeze 10 minutes.
3. Unfold pastry on a lightly floured surface. Gently roll it out. Cut in 8 equal triangles.
4. Spoon 2 teaspoons of pecan mixture onto the right side of rectangles, leaving a border. Fold left side over filling and seal edges with a fork. Pierce the tops of each pie.
5. Place half the pies in the fryer basket and put it on the baking pan. Set oven to air fryer on 375°F for 10 minutes. Cook pies 7 minutes or until puffed and golden brown. Repeat with remaining pies. Serve warm.

Nutrition Facts Per Serving
Calories 161, Total Fat 13g, Saturated Fat 4g, Total Carbs 10g, Net Carbs 9g, Protein 1g, Sugar 7g, Fiber 1g, Sodium 62mg, Potassium 48mg, Phosphorus 24mg

Churros with Chocolate Dipping Sauce

Prep time: 25 minutes, cook time: 10 minutes, Serves: 4

7 Ingredients:
- 1 ½ cup water, divided
- ¼ cup + 1 tsp butter, unsalted
- ¼ cup + 1 tsp sugar
- 1 cup flour
- 2 eggs
- 1/8 tsp salt
- 1 cup dark chocolate (60-70% cocoa solids), chopped

Instructions
1. Lightly spray baking pan with cooking spray.
2. In a saucepan, combine 1 cup water, ¼ cup butter, and 1 teaspoon sugar. Cook over medium heat until butter has melted, stirring frequently.
3. Add the flour and stir quickly to form a loose paste. Reduce heat to low and cook, stirring, until mixture starts to come away from sides of pan and firm up. Remove from heat and let cool 10 minutes.
4. Beat in eggs and salt until combined, mixture should be smooth and glossy. Transfer to a pastry bag fitted with a star shaped nozzle.
5. Pipe mixture into any shape desired on the baking pan. Place the pan in position 2 and set oven to air fry on 390°F for 6 minutes. Cook until crisp and golden brown. Repeat with remaining batter.
6. Place the chocolate, remaining water, and sugar in a double boiler. Let sit until chocolate and sugar melts completely, stirring occasionally.
7. When the mixture is melted and smooth, stir in butter and continue cooking until melted and combined. Serve immediately with churros.

Nutrition Facts Per Serving
Calories 638, Total Fat 36g, Saturated Fat 20g, Total Carbs 66g, Net Carbs 61g, Protein 10g, Sugar 33g, Fiber 5g, Sodium 211mg, Potassium 393mg, Phosphorus 234mg

Simple Cinnamon Rolls

Prep time: 10 minutes, cook time: 10 minutes, Serves: 8

8 Ingredients:
- Nonstick cooking spray
- 1 tbsp. cinnamon
- ¾ stick butter, soft
- 6 tbsp. brown sugar
- 1 sheet puff pastry, thawed
- ½ cup powdered sugar
- 1 tbsp. milk
- 2 tsp fresh lemon juice

Instructions
1. Place baking pan in position 2. Lightly spray fryer basket with cooking spray.
2. In a small bowl, stir together cinnamon, butter, and sugar.
3. Gently roll out pastry and spread with cinnamon mixture covering it completely.
4. Carefully roll up the pastry, starting at the short end. Use a serrated knife to cut the pastry in 1-inch pieces.
5. Place them in the fryer basket, these will need to be cooked in 2 batches. Place the basket on the baking pan and set oven to air fry on 400°F for 8 minutes. Cook cinnamon rolls until puffed and golden brown. Repeat with remaining rolls.
6. Let cool slightly. In a small bowl, whisk together powdered sugar, milk, and lemon juice, drizzle over cinnamon rolls and serve.

Nutrition Facts Per Serving
Calories 155, Total Fat 11g, Saturated Fat 6g, Total Carbs 13g, Net Carbs 12g, Protein 1g, Sugar 10g, Fiber 1g, Sodium 85mg, Potassium 19mg, Phosphorus 9mg

Crispy Coated Peaches

Prep time: 10 minutes, cook time: 10 minutes, Serves: 1

8 Ingredients:
- Nonstick cooking spray
- ¼ cup panko bread crumbs
- 1 tsp sugar
- ¼ tsp cinnamon
- 1/8 tsp salt
- 2 egg whites
- ¼ tsp vanilla
- 1 peach, pitted and cut in ½-inch thick slices

Instructions
1. Place baking pan in position 2. Lightly spray fryer basket with cooking spray.
2. In a medium bowl, combine bread crumbs, sugar, cinnamon, and salt.
3. In a separate medium bowl, whisk together egg whites and vanilla.
4. Add peaches to egg mixture and stir to coat. One at a time, shake off excess egg and coat with crumb mixture. Place in basket in a single layer.
5. Place basket on the baking pan and set oven to air fry on 390°F for 8 minutes. Cook until golden brown and crispy. Serve immediately topped with yogurt or whip cream.

Nutrition Facts Per Serving
Calories 222, Total Fat 2g, Saturated Fat 0g, Total Carbs 39g, Net Carbs 35g, Protein 12g, Sugar 19g, Fiber 4g, Sodium 617mg, Potassium 450mg, Phosphorus 85mg

Chapter 8 – Snacks & Appetizers

Beef Enchilada Dip

Prep time: 5 minutes, cook time: 10 minutes, Serves: 8

6 Ingredients:
- 2 lbs. ground beef
- ½ onion, chopped fine
- 2 cloves garlic, chopped fine
- 2 cups enchilada sauce
- 2 cups Monterrey Jack cheese, grated
- 2 tbsp. sour cream

Instructions
1. Place rack in position 1.
2. Heat a large skillet over med-high heat. Add beef and cook until it starts to brown. Drain off fat.
3. Stir in onion and garlic and cook until tender, about 3 minutes. Stir in enchilada sauce and transfer mixture to a small casserole dish and top with cheese.
4. Set oven to convection bake on 325°F for 10 minutes. After 5 minutes, add casserole to the oven and bake 3-5 minutes until cheese is melted and mixture is heated through.
5. Serve warm topped with sour cream.

Nutrition Facts Per Serving
Calories 414, Total Fat 22g, Saturated Fat 10g, Total Carbs 15g, Net Carbs 11g, Protein 39g, Sugar 8g, Fiber 4g, Sodium 1155mg, Potassium 635mg, Phosphorus 385mg

Cheesy Stuffed Sliders

Prep time: 15 minutes, cook time: 50 minutes, Serves: 10

6 Ingredients:
- 2 tbsp. garlic powder
- 1 ½ tsp salt
- 2 tsp pepper
- 2 lbs. ground beef
- 8 oz. mozzarella slices, cut in 20 small pieces
- 20 potato slider rolls

Instructions
1. Place baking pan in position 2.
2. In a small bowl, combine garlic powder, salt, and pepper.
3. Use 1 ½ tablespoons ground beef per patty. Roll it into a ball and press an indentation in the ball with your thumb.
4. Place a piece of cheese into beef and fold over sides to cover it completely. Flatten to ½-inch thick by 3-inches wide. Season both sides with garlic mixture.
5. Place patties in fryer basket in a single layer and place on the baking pan. Set oven to air fry on 350°F for 10 minutes. Turn patties over halfway through cooking time. Repeat with any remaining patties.
6. Place patties on bottoms of rolls and top with your favorite toppings. Serve immediately.

Nutrition Facts Per Serving
Calories 402, Total Fat 14g, Saturated Fat 5g, Total Carbs 31g, Net Carbs 29g, Protein 38g, Sugar 3g, Fiber 2g, Sodium 835mg, Potassium 397mg, Phosphorus 400mg

Philly Egg Rolls

Prep time: 10 minutes, cook time: 25 minutes, Serves: 6

11 Ingredients:
- Nonstick cooking spray
- ½ lb. lean ground beef
- ¼ tsp garlic powder
- ¼ tsp onion powder
- ¼ tsp salt
- ¼ tsp pepper
- ¾ cup green bell pepper, chopped
- ¾ cup onion, chopped
- 2 slices provolone cheese, torn into pieces
- 3 tbsp. cream cheese
- 6 square egg roll wrappers

Instructions
1. Place baking pan in position 2. Lightly spray fryer basket with cooking spray.
2. Heat a large skillet over med-high heat. Add beef, garlic powder, onion powder, salt and pepper. Stir to combine.
3. Add in bell pepper and onion and cook, stirring occasionally, until beef is no longer pink and vegetables are tender, about 6-8 minutes.
4. Remove from heat and drain fat. Add provolone and cream cheese and stir until melted and combined. Transfer to a large bowl.
5. Lay egg roll wrappers, one at a time, on a dry work surface. Spoon about 1/3 cup mixture in a row just below the center of the wrapper. Moisten edges with water. Fold the sides in towards the middle and roll up around filling.
6. Place egg rolls, seam side down in fryer basket. Spray lightly with cooking spray. Place the basket in the oven and set to air fry on 400°F for 10 minutes. Cook until golden brown, turning over halfway through cooking time. Serve immediately.

Nutrition Facts Per Serving
Calories 238, Total Fat 10g, Saturated Fat 5g, Total Carbs 21g, Net Carbs 20g, Protein 16g, Sugar 1g, Fiber 1g, Sodium 412mg, Potassium 206mg, Phosphorus 160mg

Mozzarella Cheese Sticks

Prep time: 10 minutes, cook time: 10 minutes, Serves: 6

6 Ingredients:
- Nonstick cooking spray
- 12 Mozzarella cheese sticks, halved
- 2 eggs
- ½ cup flour
- 1 ½ cups Italian panko bread crumbs
- ½ cup marinara sauce

Instructions
1. Blot cheese sticks with paper towels to soak up excess moisture.
2. In a shallow dish, beat eggs.
3. Place flour in a separate shallow dish.
4. Place bread crumbs in a third shallow dish.
5. Line a baking sheet with parchment paper.
6. One at a time, dip cheese sticks in egg, then flour, back in egg and finally in bread crumbs. Place on prepared pan. Freeze 1-2 hours until completely frozen.
7. Place baking pan in position 2 of the oven. Lightly spray fryer basket with cooking spray.
8. Place cheese sticks in a single layer in the basket and place in oven. Set to air fry on 375°F for 8 minutes. Cook until nicely browned and crispy, turning over halfway through cooking time. Serve with marinara sauce for dipping.

Nutrition Facts Per Serving
Calories 199, Total Fat 3g, Saturated Fat 1g, Total Carbs 30g, Net Carbs 28g, Protein 13g, Sugar 3g, Fiber 2g, Sodium 368mg, Potassium 175mg, Phosphorus 220mg

Buffalo Quesadillas

Prep time: 5 minutes, cook time: 5 minutes, Serves: 8
7 Ingredients:
- Nonstick cooking spray
- 2 cups chicken, cooked & chopped fine
- ½ cup Buffalo wing sauce
- 2 cups Monterey Jack cheese, grated
- ½ cup green onions, sliced thin
- 8 flour tortillas, 8-inch diameter
- ¼ cup blue cheese dressing

Instructions
1. Lightly spray the baking pan with cooking spray.
2. In a medium bowl, add chicken and wing sauce and toss to coat.
3. Place tortillas, one at a time on work surface. Spread ¼ of the chicken mixture over tortilla and sprinkle with cheese and onion. Top with a second tortilla and place on the baking pan.
4. Set oven to broil on 400°F for 8 minutes. After 5 minutes place baking pan in position 2. Cook quesadillas 2-3 minutes per side until toasted and cheese has melted. Repeat with remaining ingredients.
5. Cut quesadillas in wedges and serve with blue cheese dressing or other dipping sauce.

Nutrition Facts Per Serving
Calories 376, Total Fat 20g, Saturated Fat 8g, Total Carbs 27g, Net Carbs 26g, Protein 22g, Sugar 2g, Fiber 2g, Sodium 685mg, Potassium 201mg, Phosphorus 301mg

Crispy Sausage Bites

Prep time: 5 minutes, cook time: 15 minutes, Serves: 12

7 Ingredients:
- Nonstick cooking spray
- 2 lbs. spicy pork sausage
- 1 ½ cups Bisquick
- 4 cups sharp cheddar cheese, grated
- ½ cup onion, diced fine
- 2 tsp pepper
- 2 tsp garlic, diced fine

Instructions
1. Lightly spray baking pan with cooking spray.
2. In a large bowl, combine all ingredients. Form into 1-inch balls and place on baking pan, these will need to be cooked in batches.
3. Set oven to bake on 375°F for 20 minutes. After 5 minutes, place baking pan in position 2 and cook 12-15 minutes or until golden brown. Repeat with remaining sausage bites. Serve immediately.

Nutrition Facts Per Serving
Calories 432, Total Fat 32g, Saturated Fat 13g, Total Carbs 14g, Net Carbs 14g, Protein 22g, Sugar 1g, Fiber 0g, Sodium 803mg, Potassium 286mg, Phosphorus 298mg

Puffed Asparagus Spears

Prep time: 20 minutes, cook time: 10 minutes, Serves: 10
4 Ingredients:
- Nonstick cooking spray
- 3 oz. prosciutto, sliced thin & cut in 30 long strips
- 30 asparagus spears, trimmed
- 10 (14 x 9-inch) sheets phyllo dough, thawed

Instructions
1. Place baking pan in position 2 of the oven.
2. Wrap each asparagus spear with a piece of prosciutto, like a barber pole.
3. One at a time, place a sheet of phyllo on a work surface and cut into 3 4 1/2x9-inch rectangles.
4. Place an asparagus spear across a short end and roll up. Place in a single layer in the fryer basket. Spray with cooking spray.
5. Place the basket in the oven and set to air fry on 450°F for 10 minutes. Cook until phyllo is crisp and golden, about 8-10 minutes, turning over halfway through cooking time. Repeat with remaining ingredients. Serve warm.

Nutrition Facts Per Serving
Calories 74, Total Fat 2g, Saturated Fat 0g, Total Carbs 11g, Net Carbs 10g, Protein 3g, Sugar 0g, Fiber 1g, Sodium 189mg, Potassium 60mg, Phosphorus 33mg

Wonton Poppers

Prep time: 15 minutes, cook time: 10 minutes, Serves: 10

5 Ingredients:
- Nonstick cooking spray
- 1 package refrigerated square wonton wrappers
- 1 8-ounce package cream cheese, softened
- 3 jalapenos, seeds and ribs removed, finely chopped
- 1/2 cup shredded cheddar cheese

Instructions

1. Place baking pan in position 2 of the oven. Lightly spray fryer basket with cooking spray.
2. In a large bowl, combine all ingredients except the wrappers until combined.
3. Lay wrappers in a single layer on a baking sheet. Spoon a teaspoon of filling in the center. Moisten the edges with water and fold wrappers over filling, pinching edges to seal. Place in a single layer in the basket.
4. Place the basket in the oven and set to air fry on 375°F for 10 minutes. Cook until golden brown and crisp, turning over halfway through cooking time. Repeat with remaining ingredients. Serve immediately.

Nutrition Facts Per Serving
Calories 287, Total Fat 11g, Saturated Fat 6g, Total Carbs 38g, Net Carbs 37g, Protein 9g, Sugar 1g, Fiber 1g, Sodium 485mg, Potassium 98mg, Phosphorus 104mg

Party Pull Apart

Prep time: 15 minutes, cook time: 20 minutes, Serves: 10

7 Ingredients:
- 5 cloves garlic
- 1/3 cup fresh parsley
- 2 tbsp. olive oil
- 4 oz. mozzarella cheese, sliced
- 3 tbsp. butter
- 1/8 tsp salt
- 1 loaf sour dough bread

Instructions
1. Place the rack in position 1 of the oven.
2. In a food processor, add garlic, parsley, and oil and pulse until garlic is chopped fine.
3. Stack the mozzarella cheese and cut into 1-inch squares.
4. Heat the butter in a small saucepan over medium heat. Add the garlic mixture and salt and cook 2 minutes, stirring occasionally. Remove from heat.
5. Use a sharp, serrated knife to make 1-inch diagonal cuts across the bread being careful not to cut all the way through.
6. With a spoon, drizzle garlic butter into the cuts in the bread. Stack 3-4 cheese squares and place in each of the cuts.
7. Place the bread on a sheet of foil and fold up the sides. Cut a second piece of foil just big enough to cover the top.
8. Set oven to convection bake on 350°F for 25 minutes. After 5 minutes, place the bread in the oven and bake 10 minutes.
9. Remove the top piece of foil and bake 10 minutes more until the cheese has completely melted. Serve immediately.

Nutrition Facts Per Serving
Calories 173, Total Fat 7g, Saturated Fat 3g, Total Carbs 18g, Net Carbs 17g, Protein 7g, Sugar 2g, Fiber 1g, Sodium 337mg, Potassium 68mg, Phosphorus 112mg

Easy Cheesy Stuffed Mushrooms

Prep time 10 minutes, cook time: 15 minutes, Serves: 4

7 Ingredients:
- Nonstick cooking spray
- 1/3 cup cream cheese, soft
- 1 tbsp. parmesan cheese, grated
- ¼ tsp garlic salt
- 2 tbsp. spinach, thaw, press dry & chop
- 8 oz. mushrooms, rinsed & stems removed
- 1 tbsp. panko bread crumbs

Instructions
1. Lightly spray baking sheet with cooking spray.
2. In a medium bowl, combine cream cheese, parmesan, salt, and spinach, mix well.
3. Place mushrooms on baking sheet and fill with cheese mixture. Sprinkle bread crumbs over top.
4. Set oven to bake on 350°F for 20 minutes. After 5 minutes, place baking pan in position 2 of the oven and cook mushrooms 15 minutes until tops are lightly browned. Serve hot.

Nutrition Facts Per Serving

Calories 121, Total Fat 7g, Saturated Fat 4g, Total Carbs 8g, Net Carbs 7g, Protein 4g, Sugar 2g, Fiber 1g, Sodium 168mg, Potassium 225mg, Phosphorus 86mg

www.ingramcontent.com/pod-product-compliance
Lightning Source LLC
Chambersburg PA
CBHW081122080526
44587CB00021B/3719